MILESTONES
IN
AMERICAN HISTORY
★ ★ ★ ★ ★ ★ ★ ★ ★ ★ ★ ★ ★ ★ ★

THE TREATY OF PARIS
THE PRECURSOR TO A NEW NATION

MILESTONES
IN
AMERICAN HISTORY

THE TREATY OF PARIS

THE MONROE DOCTRINE

THE TRANSCONTINENTAL RAILROAD

THE ELECTRIC LIGHT

THE WRIGHT BROTHERS

THE STOCK MARKET CRASH OF 1929

SPUTNIK/EXPLORER I

THE CIVIL RIGHTS ACT OF 1964

MILESTONES
IN AMERICAN HISTORY

THE TREATY OF PARIS

THE PRECURSOR TO A NEW NATION

EDWARD J. RENEHAN JR.

CHELSEA HOUSE
PUBLISHERS
An imprint of Infobase Publishing

Cover: The signing of the Treaty of Paris, which formally ended the American Revolution, is depicted in bronze on this door in France.

The Treaty of Paris: The Precursor to a New Nation

Copyright © 2007 by Infobase Publishing

Chelsea House
An imprint of Infobase Publishing
132 West 31st Street
New York, NY 10001

ISBN-10: 0-7910-9352-2
ISBN-13: 978-0-7910-9352-8

Library of Congress Cataloging-in-Publication Data
Renehan, Edward, 1956-
  The Treaty of Paris : the precursor to a new nation / Edward J. Renehan, Jr.
      p. cm. — (Milestones in American history)
  Includes bibliographical references and index.
  Audience: Grades 9-12.
  ISBN 0-7910-9352-2 (hardcover)
  1. United States—History—Revolution, 1775–1783—Peace—Juvenile literature. 2. Great Britain. Treaties, etc. United States, 1783 Sept. 3—Juvenile literature. I. Title. II. Series.
  E249.R46 2007
  973.3'17—dc22   2006034129

Chelsea House books are available at special discounts when purchased in bulk quantities for businesses, associations, institutions, or sales promotions. Please call our Special Sales Department in New York at (212) 967-8800 or (800) 322-8755.

You can find Chelsea House on the World Wide Web at http://www.chelseahouse.com

Series design by Erik Lindstrom
Cover design by Ben Peterson

Printed in the United States of America

Bang FOF 10 9 8 7 6 5 4 3 2 1

This book is printed on acid-free paper.

All links and Web addresses were checked and verified to be correct at the time of publication. Because of the dynamic nature of the Web, some addresses and links may have changed since publication and may no longer be valid.

CONTENTS

Birth of a Nation

It was a sunny, warm day in Paris, September 3, 1783. U.S. representatives John Adams of Massachusetts, Benjamin Franklin of Pennsylvania, and John Jay of New York (accompanied by Henry Laurens of Carolina) sat down in a small suite at Paris's Hotel d'York on the Rue Jacob, to sign a treaty ending hostilities between the United States and Great Britain: the war for U.S. independence. Representing and signing the documents for King George III and the British Parliament was a glum David Hartley, a diplomat and member of Parliament. Others in the British party included an equally solemn Richard Oswald, who had signed the first draft of the treaty the previous November, prior to its ratification by Congress and Parliament. The reason the ceremony took place in the small hotel suite was simple. Although the Americans had lobbied to hold the signing at the grand palace of Versailles, Hartley had

On September 3, 1783, American representatives John Adams, Benjamin Franklin, and John Jay signed the Treaty of Paris, which formally ended the American Revolution. Pictured here are the signatures of the three representatives, which follow Article X of the document.

insisted that he did not want to travel so far from town. Thus, history was made at this far more humble setting.

Courtiers and assistants bustled busily about the men. Among the secretaries was Franklin's own grandson, who, along with the others, copied documents for the proceedings. Butlers brought tea and, for Franklin, something a little stronger. Franklin was the senior member of the delegation and, in the eyes of some, had done the least to bring the treaty to this point. He nevertheless spoke loudly and at length about the greatness and solemnity of this occasion. His country, he announced, was now finally coming into its own as a recognized nation-state. This day, the eloquent Franklin insisted, was not only a pivotal one for America, but for the world—indeed, for all mankind.

Franklin was right to be exuberant, just as the British were right, from their side, to be somewhat less than thrilled. To say the least, the terms of the treaty were generous to the new government of the United States. In essence, the treaty achieved for the former colonies virtually every war aim originally spelled out by Congress at the start of the American Revolution. These included expansive borders, fishing rights off Newfoundland in Canada, and the pledge that the British would eventually remove all their troops from the United States. The treaty also made navigation of the Mississippi River free to all signatories, and restored Florida to Spain and Senegal (in West Africa) to France. True, a few issues—such as the precise latitude of the United States' northeastern border—remained to be debated by future negotiators. But in the end, the U.S. representatives, together with their Congress, were delighted with the settlement that, most importantly, recognized the independence of the United States and its place among the community of nations.

A few weeks after the signing, Franklin corresponded with his British friend Jonathan Shipley. "Let us forgive and forget," he wrote. "Let each country seek its advancement in its own internal advantages of arts and agriculture, not in retarding or preventing the prosperity of the other. America will, with God's blessing, become a great and happy country; and England, if she has at length gained wisdom, will have gained something more valuable, and more essential to her prosperity, than all she has lost." At about the same time, to another British friend (Richard Price), Franklin wrote: "Our [America's] Revolution is an important event for the advantage of mankind in general. . . . Liberty, which some years since appeared in danger of extinction, is now regaining the ground she had lost." Franklin went on to note that "arbitrary governments" were likely in the future to become "more mild and reasonable, and to expire by degrees." Elsewhere, Franklin added: "After much occasion to consider the folly and mischiefs of a state of warfare, and the little or no advantage obtained by those nations who have conducted it with the most success, I have been apt to think that there has never been, nor ever will be, any such thing as a *good* war, or a *bad* peace."

EVOLVING CAST

The document the men signed would, in the following years, be called the "Treaty of Paris," the "Paris Peace Treaty," or, on occasion, the "Second Treaty of Paris." Although the first descriptive phrase is more common, the last is more accurate. Twenty years before the treaty ending the American Revolution, the "first" Treaty of Paris had ended the French and Indian War and the Seven Years' War. With that treaty—signed by Great Britain, France, and Spain—France lost to Great Britain all of its North American possessions (except Louisiana, which it had ceded to Spain). The treaty likewise excluded French troops from Bengal, effectively ending the French imperial drive into India. In addition, in Africa, France yielded Senegal to Great Britain. The only colonies retained by France were Saint Pierre and Miquelon (in the Gulf of Saint Lawrence in Canada); Saint Lucia, Haiti, Guadeloupe, and Martinique (in the West Indies); and Pondicherry and Chandernagor (in India). Spain recovered Cuba and the Philippines but ceded Florida to Great Britain. Thus, the 1763 Treaty of Paris greatly enlarged the territory of the British Empire, just as the Second Treaty of Paris greatly diminished it.

The U.S. commissioners signing the second treaty could not have been more aware of this fact.

The cast of characters in the U.S. commission changed through the years of the revolutionary era. At first, in 1776, the commission at Paris consisted of Franklin, Silas Deane of Connecticut, and Arthur Lee of Virginia. John Adams of Massachusetts arrived to replace Deane—who was recalled by Congress—in April 1778. A few months after this, on September 14, 1778, Franklin found himself appointed sole ambassador to France, thus replacing the commission and unwittingly insulting and infuriating both Lee and Adams. (Franklin presented his credentials, those documents having been slow to travel across the Atlantic Ocean, on March 23, 1779.) Later that same year, 1779, Adams was put in charge of negotiating treaties of peace and commerce with Great Britain. In June 1781, the Continental Congress put together a "Peace Commission" of Adams, Franklin, John Jay, Henry Laurens, and Thomas Jefferson of Virginia, effectively taking back Adams's original sole responsibility for the task. Once again, Adams felt himself to have been blindsided by the territorial Franklin, who seemed intent on owning a piece of virtually every major diplomatic initiative.

Just as the American cast had changed through time, so had their mission. At first, the commissioners had been charged with securing treaties of commerce and alliance with France, and to acquire French financial aid. Also, their orders from home commanded them to acquire and ship supplies for the American Army, and to arrange assistance and protection for American naval vessels in French waters. They were also asked to set up the commissioning of privateers, hired pirates who worked legally for governments. The commissioners promoted

The 1763 Treaty of Paris, which officially ended the Seven Years' War, enlarged Great Britain's territory in North America. This 1775 map of Great Britain's American colonies illustrates its land holdings. Prior to the 1763 treaty, France held much of Canada and the territory west of the Allegheny Mountains.

the exchange and return of American prisoners of war, and—on the stage of public relations—worked to foster the sympathy and support of the French court and French people for the American cause. After the war became an international event and the British began to actively seek an exit from the conflict, the American group (or the *commission*, as it was called) was ordered to seek peace with Great Britain. The peace was finally made official in 1783 in that modest hotel room in Paris, with only waiters to serve as witness.

THE STORY OF A PORTRAIT

The treaty negotiations had been complex, to say the least. By the spring of 1782, the war that had started on Lexington Green in 1775 had spread to the shores of Europe, Africa, Central America, the Caribbean, and throughout the Mediterranean Sea and Indian Ocean. No longer simply an attempt by American colonials to secure their independence, the American Revolution eventually came to engage the military and naval forces of much of Europe. One war became four, each of them waged against Great Britain. England was fighting against, in turn, America (seeking independence), France (seeking to improve its position in the European balance of power), Spain (seeking to recover possessions seized by the British in earlier wars), and the Netherlands (asserting trading rights). All these wars had accumulated into one big headache for Parliament and King George III. (The Spanish siege of Gibraltar, for example, had forced the British to divert troops and ships from the American front.)

As diplomatic problems, however, each little war had a life of its own. From a technical point of view, America was not even an ally of Spain or the Netherlands. Nevertheless, treaties had to be negotiated at the same time among all parties in order for hostilities to cease in a meaningful and permanent way. The complexities of this situation made the peace talks of 1782 to 1783, in Paris and elsewhere, among the most challenging diplomatic exercises in history. It also made for bruised

George III reigned as king of England from 1760 to 1801 and saw his North American empire expand after the Seven Years' War, but then diminish in size after the American Revolution. King George is depicted in full military uniform in this 1800 painting by British artist Sir William Beechey.

egos, shattered friendships, and wounded pride on the parts of those crafting the peace.

On the day of the final treaty signing, American painter Benjamin West attempted to have the principal negotiators pose for a portrait. All the Americans—victorious, triumphant—immediately agreed. The British, however, dawdled and in the end did not show up to pose. Hartley and Oswald had no interest in immortalizing their empire's moment of abject defeat at the hands of squalid colonials. They did not think it a day worth remembering on canvas.

Thus, West captured only the Americans. His half-finished painting exists to this day. The portrait shows John Jay, John Adams, Benjamin Franklin, and the less-involved Henry Laurens (who arrived on the scene too late to actively engage in the negotiations), along with Franklin's secretary and grandson, William Temple Franklin. The Americans look contented, but serious. They are hardly jovial, despite the festivity of the occasion. Why is that?

The answer perhaps lies in the fact that serious differences of opinion and personal feelings of ill will alienated Jay, Adams, and Laurens from Franklin. To all of them, especially Adams, Franklin had seemed overly influenced by the French, especially Foreign Minister Charles Gravier, count de Vergennes. Almost all the various American diplomats in France tended to dislike and distrust Franklin, branding him as immoral, lazy, careless in the discharge of duties, excessively vain, and too admiring of the French. In a letter, Adams described Franklin as "selfish . . . and eaten with all the passions which prey upon old age unprincipled." Adams wrote that Franklin believed "the United States ought to join France in two future wars against [Great Britain]—the first to pay the debt we owe her [France] for making war for us. And the second to show ourselves as generous as she had been. It is high time his resignation was accepted. He has done mischief enough. He has been possessed by the lowest cunning and the deepest hypocrisy I ever met."

Adams frowned on Franklin's frequent womanizing, and his love of fine wines and large dinners. In fact, Adams found offensive the luxuries of French aristocrats in general—luxuries cherished by Franklin. Adams and Jay loudly questioned the motives of America's French allies, and sought to negotiate directly with the British to the exclusion of French interests during the treaty talks. Franklin, though, had consistently insisted on American loyalty to the French. He proved indispensable near the end of the process, soothing French nerves and reactions after Jay and Adams concluded a separate peace, this to be followed by separate documents ending Great Britain's wars with the other powers. Jay and Adams and Franklin played equally vital roles in the complex negotiations that led to the 1783 Treaty of Paris. In the end, despite themselves—and especially despite Adams and Franklin—they proved a good team, a well-matched assembly of American representatives.

Still, Jay, Laurens, and Adams appear a bit uncomfortable in their portraits. They look as though they would rather, at that moment, be standing far from Franklin and his grandson. In fact, they look as though they would rather be anywhere else than with the Franklins. Four months after the signing in Paris, Jay and Adams would thaw just a bit and break bread with Franklin in Annapolis, Maryland. The occasion was to celebrate the final ratification of the signed treaty by Congress, which at the time was meeting in Annapolis. After the vote, the three founding fathers would retreat to a restaurant (an establishment still in business, known as the Treaty of Paris Restaurant) to make merry and, despite lingering animosities and prejudices, congratulate one another on a job well done.

Today, Benjamin West's original portrait painting—or at least the half that he was able to complete—can be seen at the Winterthur Museum and Country Estate in northern Delaware. The State Department in Washington, D.C., has a copy on display that many people wrongly believe to be the original. Nevertheless, the copy is a good one and is revered

American artist Benjamin West's famous rendition of the American representatives (left to right: John Jay, John Adams, Benjamin Franklin, Henry
Laurens, and William Temple Franklin) at the Treaty of Paris is on display at
Winterthur Museum and Country Estate in northern Delaware. West did not
finish the painting, because the British commissioners refused to pose.

by modern-day diplomats and ambassadors as representing
the very first formal act of diplomacy on the part of the new
American nation. From a diplomatic point of view, the history of the United States begins with the signing of the Treaty
of Paris in September 1783. As all engaged in representing the
United States abroad know, that little, understated ceremony of

signing held so long ago at the Hotel d'York signaled the launch of the republic on the world stage.

Though rarely told or examined at length, the story of the Treaty of Paris—how it came about, the many fascinating conflicts between the brilliant personalities who shaped it, and the troubled environment in which it was negotiated—forms one of the most important chapters in the tale of the birth of the United States. The tale is a study in statecraft, personal and political intrigue, and personal and international brinkmanship. It is also a story of decadence, bitter individual jealousies and rivalries, and brilliant minds engaged in high-stakes intellectual battles on which the fate of a nation depended.

First Seeds
of Peace

As has been mentioned, the Continental Congress appointed the first so-called "Peace Commission" in June 1781. This commission consisted of John Adams—previously appointed sole negotiator for the matters with Great Britain—along with John Jay, Benjamin Franklin, Henry Laurens, and Thomas Jefferson. Jefferson, despite being named in the documents, would play no active role because he was already busy with other assignments. The peace demands, as spelled out by Congress, were limited to *independence* and *sovereignty*, giving the committee discretion on such issues as boundaries, fishing rights, and navigation of the Mississippi River.

AUSPICIOUS MOMENT

It was an optimistic time for peace. For seven years, King George III and the government of Lord Frederick North had tried without success to put down the American rebellion. But every brief moment of success had inevitably been followed by defeat for the British, who found themselves beaten at Bunker Hill, Trenton, and Saratoga. Then, finally, came British general Charles Cornwallis's greatest humiliation: the fight at Yorktown.

The stage for the Battle of Yorktown was set after the Battle of Guilford Courthouse on March 15, 1781. The British debacle began when General Cornwallis ignored instructions from his superior, General Sir Henry Clinton, who wanted Cornwallis to use his battle-weary troops to defend British outposts in the Carolinas. Instead, Cornwallis brought his men to Virginia, where he took over command from General Benedict Arnold, the famous American traitor. At the same time, General George Washington was planning an invasion of British-held New York. Noting Cornwallis's shift to Virginia, Washington sent his French ally, Gilbert du Motier, marquis de Lafayette, to that same terrain in the spring of 1781, with several Continental Army regiments. Washington thereafter reinforced Lafayette's group through June, at which point Cornwallis pulled back to the Yorktown Peninsula. Once again disobeying a direct order from General Clinton, who told him to send all of his 7,500 men to New York, Cornwallis stayed where he was and began preparing to defend Yorktown and Yorktown's sister city of Gloucester, on the other side of the York River.

In due course, Washington and the French general Rochambeau, with 2,500 Continental and 4,000 French troops between them, started toward Virginia, where they joined Lafayette's men to form a mass of 16,000 troops. Meanwhile, Admiral François Joseph Paul de Grasse arrived with his French fleet at Chesapeake Bay on August 30. Admiral de Grasse effectively trapped Cornwallis between the large assembly of French and American land forces and the equally massive French fleet. Outnumbered, surrounded, and running out of supplies, Cornwallis surrendered, disgraced, on October 19, 1781.

On October 19, 1781, British general Charles Cornwallis surrendered to American and French forces at Yorktown, Virginia, effectively ending the American Revolution. This Currier and Ives rendition of the surrender depicts Cornwallis handing his sword over to George Washington, the commander of the American forces.

Thereafter, most reasonable men on both sides of the Atlantic realized the American rebellion had achieved its goals. All there remained to do was formalize this fact in writing.

OVERTURE

At Paris, Benjamin Franklin did not receive news of the British surrender at Yorktown until a month after the fact. Elkanah Watson, an American merchant and friend of Franklin's, who happened to be visiting Franklin's apartment in Passy, a suburb of Paris, tells the tale in his diary. On the evening of November 19, before receiving word of the events at Yorktown, Franklin and his visitors discussed

> the grand military combination of America and France to subdue the army of Cornwallis, in Virginia. . . . We weighed the probabilities—balanc'd vicissitudes—dissected the best maps. . . . As Franklin's great influence at the Court of France was the primary cause of producing this bold enterprise, it can be easily conceived how strong must have been his excitements in our alternate views of probable results.
>
> At times his Philosophy seem'd to abandon him in gloomy despondency—& then viewing the issue in an opposite light, his hopes wou'd flash into a concertion [sic] of complete success. Altho' in his 76th year, yet his whole machinery appeared in a state of elasticity, and in active play—So much was he exhilerated [sic] when hope predominated.

After these discussions, Watson went back to his hotel late in the evening "in gloomy despondency." But he was glad to be awakened a few hours later by a messenger from Franklin, carrying word of the victory. Watson said of it:

> The same day I waited on his Excellency with many American & French to Offer our congratulations. He appeared in an ecstacy [sic] of joy, observing, "there is no parallel in history

of two entire armies being captured from the same enemy in any one war." . . . The American character now rose to an enviable height—the joy of all classes of people was excessive. Paris was brilliantly illuminated three successive nights on this glorious occasion—which settles our controversy definitively with England. On my return to Nantes I found all the Cities in my rout in a blaze of illumination.

Franklin told Watson that it would now be just a matter of waiting for the British to make a move and open up negotiations. And wait he did, until the following March, at which point Franklin—tired of inaction—took the initiative. During March 1782, Franklin wrote the Earl of Shelburne, an old friend of his who was known to favor American interests and whose political fortunes seemed to be on the rise in London. Commenting on the generally improving British political situation, Franklin added: "I hope it will tend to produce a general Peace, which I am persuaded your Lordship, with all good Men, desires, which I wish to see before I die, & to which I shall with infinite Pleasure contribute every thing in my Power."

Thus the peace negotiations, however informally, were launched. "It didn't need much more than a hint," wrote historian Jonathan Dull.

FRANKLIN TAKES THE LEAD

April 1782 found John Adams at the Hague in the Netherlands. He had spent much time there in the previous two years, empowered by Congress to raise Dutch loans to finance the American Revolution, to conclude a commercial treaty, and to work toward formal Dutch recognition of the former 13 colonies as an independent nation. Throughout 1780, Adams had written a series of letters meant for publication to his Dutch friend Hendrik Calkoen, explaining the origins, progress, and nature of the American Revolution. One year later, Adams presented a lengthy report to the States General of the United

Provinces, calling on the Dutch government to recognize and conclude a commercial treaty with America. Then he published the document as a pamphlet in English, French, and Dutch. Finally, in April 1782, after these efforts, in addition to much personal diplomacy on Adams's part in Amsterdam, the Dutch government officially recognized the 13 rebellious colonies of America as an independent state. The same window of time found John Jay in Spain, where he had been serving as minister to the Spanish Court since 1779, working on obtaining support for and recognition of American independence. Early on, there had been hope that Jay might succeed. The monarchies of Spain and France made common cause through the edicts of the Bourbon Family Compact. Spain, on the one hand, nurtured old objections against Great Britain, especially British control of the most vital strategic point—access to the Mediterranean Sea at Gibraltar. During the spring of 1779, Spain agreed to join France in waging war on Great Britain. However, unlike the French, the Spanish did not demand British recognition of American independence. Nor did they commit themselves to fight until the British were off American soil. After these decisions from the Spanish Court, Jay was effectively cut off from the Court.

Why didn't the Spanish join the French in supporting the American Revolution? The answer is simple. Spain's rulers disputed American claims to lands west of the Appalachian Mountains and to navigation rights on the Mississippi River. The Spanish were also concerned that seeds of the American Revolution might spread to Spain's own colonies in the Americas. Thus, in April 1782, as Adams enjoyed his successes in Holland, Jay was feeling frustrated and worried about his unaccomplished mission in Spain.

That same month, Benjamin Franklin turned down offers from the British government to begin peace negotiations. The English wished to reach a settlement that would give the 13 colonies increased power to govern themselves, although they

**In April 1782, while he was serving as the American dip-
lomat to France, Benjamin Franklin rejected Great Britain's
initial overtures at peace. Franklin had been directed by the
Continental Congress to accept nothing less than complete
sovereignty for the colonies, and the British offer of autonomy
under their control was unacceptable.**

would still remain under the umbrella of the British Empire.
Following instructions from the Continental Congress,
Franklin made a firm demand that the British officially recognize American independence and sovereignty. He likewise
refused (although this topic would come up again) to con-

sider a peace treaty that did not involve a peace between Great Britain and France, America's new ally. However, Franklin did agree, in principle, to open negotiations with the British to discuss an end to the war.

Talks proceeded on two simultaneous tracks. Richard Oswald, an elderly British diplomat, dealt with the American end of the discussion. Meanwhile, Thomas Grenville, a young British aristocrat, dealt with French foreign minister Count de Vergennes, who also represented the interests of Spain. Behind the scenes of the talks, Grenville argued that America and the Crown should come to a peace not linked to the British negotiations with the French. Although Franklin sent for Adams and Jay to join him in the discussions, he did not wait for the arrival of his fellow peace commissioners before he dove into complex conversations with one too many British representatives.

Oswald and Grenville reported to different superiors in the British government. Oswald worked for the colonial secretary, Franklin's friend the Earl of Shelburne, while Grenville worked for the foreign secretary, Charles James Fox. Shelburne and Fox had completely different priorities and agendas. Shelburne sought to move slowly. The colonial secretary still hoped to reach a compromise with the Americans, one that would maintain at least some link between Great Britain and its former colonies. Fox, on the other hand, believed Great Britain should grant immediate and unconditional independence to the colonies. For starters, he argued bluntly, the colonies were basically independent already, having sent the British military running for cover. Secondly, by promptly formalizing American independence, Fox believed the British could break the alliance between the French and the Americans. Once that occurred, Fox planned to abandon the talks between Grenville and Vergennes, and fall upon France, Spain, and the Netherlands with the full might of British naval power.

DEBT AND GRATITUDE

Early on, Grenville sought a meeting with Franklin in order to repeat the proposition of a separate peace between Great Britain and America, to the exclusion of France. In doing so, he was following explicit instructions issued by Fox:

> After having seen Mons. De Vergennes you will go to Dr. Franklin, to whom you will hold the same language as to the former, and as far as his country is concerned there can be no difficulty in shewing [sic] him that there is no longer any subject of dispute and that if unhappily this treaty should break off his countrymen will be engaged in a war in which they can have no interest whatever either immediate or remote. It will be very material that, during your stay at Paris, and in the various opportunities you may have of conversing with this gentleman, you should endeavor to discover whether, if the treaty should break off or be found impracticable on account of points in which America has no concern, there may not in that case be a prospect of a separate peace between G. Britain and America, which after such an event must be so evidently for the mutual interests of both countries.

But Franklin rebuffed such talk from young Grenville. In fact, upon hearing Grenville's messages, the American diplomat immediately escorted the Brit to a joint meeting with Vergennes. During that meeting, Grenville accused the French of provoking the Americans to revolt, and claimed that the blame for all the bloodshed of recent years laid with France. "On which," Franklin was to recall, "the Count de Vergennes grew a little warm, and declared, firmly, that the breach was made, and our independence declared, long before we received the least encouragement from France; and he defied the world to give the smallest proof of the contrary. 'There sits,' said he,

'Mr. Franklin, who knows the fact, and can contradict me if I do not speak the truth.'"

Grenville determinedly followed Franklin back to his apartment. Running behind the esteemed gentleman from

BENJAMIN FRANKLIN
(1706–1790)

Polymath

Born in Boston in 1706, Ben Franklin was an American statesman, printer, scientist, inventor, and writer. The only American of the colonial period to earn an international reputation as a natural philosopher, he is best remembered today as a patriot and diplomat. Franklin left school at 10 years of age to help his father, a maker of candles and soap. He was later apprenticed to his half brother James, printer and publisher of the *New England Courant,* to which young Ben secretly contributed. Later on, he left the job with his brother and in 1723 went to Philadelphia to establish himself as a printer. Following a period in London (1724–26), Franklin returned to the colonies. In 1729, he acquired an interest in the *Pennsylvania Gazette.*

Franklin's initial success in publishing the *Gazette* led him to also publish additional periodicals, including *General Magazine* and—most notably—*Poor Richard's Almanack.* The numerous proverbs of Poor Richard, which encouraged common sense, thrift, honesty, healthy living, and general wisdom, have become standard sayings in American speech. Franklin started a debating club that eventually became the American Philosophical Society. He helped establish a small academy destined to evolve into the University of Pennsylvania. And he brought about numerous civic reforms and innovations. His many writings are still widely known and respected today, especially his autobiography, which is considered a classic of American literature.

Hungry for all forms of knowledge, Franklin made a lifelong habit of studying languages, philosophy, and science. He improved on the

Philadelphia, Grenville insisted that America had accomplished its goal and achieved independence; thus the former colonies had no more need to continue fighting than they had need for maintaining their alliance with the French.

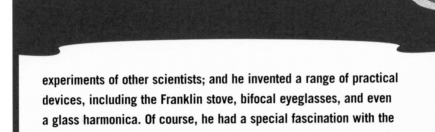

experiments of other scientists; and he invented a range of practical devices, including the Franklin stove, bifocal eyeglasses, and even a glass harmonica. Of course, he had a special fascination with the phenomenon of electricity. His famous experiment of flying a kite in a thunderstorm has been much discussed, as has his invention of the lightning rod.

As the events leading to the American Revolution came to a head, Franklin almost immediately became one of the leading statesmen and diplomats involved with the fledgling republic. Franklin served as a delegate to the Continental Congress, and as postmaster general, the official in charge of the postal service. He traveled to Canada with Continental Congress members Samuel Chase and Charles Carroll to attempt to persuade the people there to support the patriot cause. During 1776, he served on the committee that drafted the Declaration of Independence. Later that same year, Franklin sailed to France to join Arthur Lee and Silas Deane in their diplomatic efforts.

After his long adventure helping to negotiate the Treaty of Paris, Franklin returned to the United States, where he was president of the Pennsylvania Executive Council. Toward the end of his life, Franklin played a key role in the Federal Constitutional Convention of 1787. During that conference, Franklin proposed a single-house congress (as opposed to the two houses at work today) and a weak executive council. Neither of those ideas received approval. Still, he played a key role in the drafting of the final document, and he lobbied strenuously for its adoption in its final form. Franklin died in his adopted city of Philadelphia in 1790, where he is buried today.

Franklin's response, sent a few days later, was an essay on debt and gratitude:

> A, a stranger to B, sees him about to be imprisoned for a debt by a merciless creditor. He lends him the sum necessary to preserve his liberty. B then becomes the debtor of A and, after some time, repays the money. Has he then discharged the obligation? No. He has discharged the financial debt, but the obligation remains, and he is a debtor for the kindness of A, in lending him the sum so seasonably. If B should afterwards find A in the same circumstances that he, B, had been in when A lent him the money, he may then discharge this obligation or debt of kindness, *in part*, by lending him an equal sum. *In part*, and not *wholly*, because when A lent B the money there had been no prior benefit received to induce him to it. And therefore if A should a second time need the assistance, B, if in his power, is in duty bound to afford it to him.

Grenville replied that theories of personal debt did not apply in the pragmatic world of international relations. Nation-states did not have friends; they had *interests*. To this, Franklin responded that he personally, as an American, felt an enormous personal and public debt to France, and that he believed his view to be representative of that of his countrymen. "Thus he gained nothing of the point he came to push," Franklin recalled. "We parted, however, in good humour."

Backstories
to Negotiation

While other American diplomats such as Adams and Jay would eventually quibble with Franklin's vain and frivolous personality, it was only the pathologically paranoid Arthur Lee of Virginia who questioned the diplomat's integrity and sincerity. Early in the peace talks—before Adams and Jay joined the discussions—Lee did much to question Franklin's credibility and undermine his authority. In short, Lee proved no friend to Franklin or, in the end, to American interests.

Lee loudly stated to all who would listen that Franklin was really more a representative of France than of the American colonies, holding French interests to his heart, and intent on pleasing his many French friends. Lee insisted that Franklin had only been appointed to the peace commission "by the absolute order of France" as communicated by Chevalier de la Luzerne, the French minister in Philadelphia, while "at this very

In 1776, American diplomats Arthur Lee (depicted here), Benjamin Franklin, and Silas Deane were appointed commissioners to negotiate an alliance with France and attempt to obtain aid from other European countries in the colonial war effort. Unfortunately, Lee did not get along with Franklin or Deane and was recalled from France in 1779.

time, Congress had the fullest evidence and conviction that Dr. Franklin was both a dishonest and incapable man." Lee said that Franklin was in fact working mainly for the French, and would be negotiating terms favorable to the French Court first, and favorable to the former colonies only secondly. This arrangement, said Lee, put Franklin "in the way of receiving money, which is the God of his idolatry. The yoke is riveted upon us. . . . The French therefore are to make peace for us."

Nothing could have been further from the truth. However, Lee was correct in observing that Franklin spent a great deal of time consulting with—and consorting with—Charles de Vergennes. The latter served as an important sounding board and ally in Franklin's early negotiations. He was also a friend with whom the American frequently dined and drank and socialized. Franklin enjoyed the French and their social life. He did not try to hide it, and he made no apologies.

"Your enemies industriously publish that your age and indolence have unabled [sic] you for your station," Robert Morris wrote Franklin from America, "that a sense of obligation to France seals your lips when you should ask their aid; and that (whatever your friends may say to the contrary) both your connections and influence at Court are extremely feeble." Franklin answered that he was "extremely sorry" to hear of elements in the Americas viewing the French allies with anything but praise. "It is our firm connection with France that gives us weight with England, and respect throughout Europe. If we were to break our faith with this nation, on whatever pretence, England would again trample on us, and every other nation despise us. The true political interest of America consists in observing and fulfilling with the greatest exactitude, the engagements of our alliance with France."

FRANKLIN IN PARIS

Benjamin Franklin's residence from 1777 to 1785 was at the Hôtel de Valentinois, at the intersection of Rue Raynouard and Rue Singer, in Passy, a suburb of Paris. This was an establishment owned by Franklin's friend Le Ray de Chaumont, an international merchant. In addition to housing Franklin's private apartment, the hotel also housed the small offices of the American mission to the French Court, where Franklin worked—variously, through the years—with Arthur Lee, Silas Deane, and later John Adams, John Jay, and Henry Laurens.

None of these other men, however, received the honored welcome that the French bestowed on Franklin. As Jonathan Dull points out: "Franklin . . . was treated as a professional diplomat; the other American representatives were considered amateurs." Ellen Cohn, another Franklin expert, concurs. "French support [for America] was due entirely to Franklin. In terms of world fame, there is no question that during this time Franklin was the most famous American in the world. The French adored him. There were many images of Franklin circulating at this time; there was hardly a house in France that didn't have one. Franklin himself had a part in popularizing his image when he arrived. I believe this was part of his plan to win the French over, a bit like an early spin campaign."

Whenever he was not busy with his diplomatic work, Franklin spent time with members of the Paris community who shared his interests in science and philosophy. At the same time, he used these relationships to force himself to become fluent in French. Says Cohn: "He had a really wonderful group of close friends in Passy, the suburb of Paris where he lived. Learning French with them was like a big parlor game—he would write things and they would correct them." An avid womanizer, Franklin's exercises in written French included not only scholarly essays and diplomatic and scientific arguments, but also an abundance of love letters to a variety of women.

Franklin's energetic lust for all things (knowledge, women, and financial and diplomatic success) made his personality seem particularly exciting and fascinating to the French. Franklin scholar Claude-Anne Lopez says Franklin was "a very positive man. He didn't want to appear sad or depressed. I can see why he could charm the French because at that time . . . laughing was the thing."

Lopez adds:

Franklin was active in almost every aspect of French culture. He was interested in papermaking. He got very interested

During his time in France, Benjamin Franklin cultivated relationships with some of that country's most important figures. As depicted in this painting, Franklin was very comfortable in social settings and enjoyed being the center of attention for France's aristocracy.

in [hot air] balloons. He was interested in insane asylums, making them a bit better. He was involved in making a better oven for prisoners that could bake better bread. Among his inventions was the foreign service—he was the pioneer. He got along with everybody. He was a Protestant but he gave money to the local [Catholic] church because he felt it was doing good work. He was able to do many unexpected things because he didn't know he wasn't supposed to. . . . This was his approach: "Make them like you. Make them your ally. We need their ships, we need their troops."

In the opinion of author Jonathan Dull, Franklin's seemingly random approach to things was in fact a carefully orchestrated exercise in winning the hearts and minds of the French elite.

"Though he could be frivolous, Franklin was not a frivolous person," Dull notes. "He was a patriot. He was consumed with rage at George III about the way he was conducting the war. Underneath, Franklin was a very serious person and a very angry person. His friendship with France was a means to an end, though he enjoyed his time there."

Franklin was invited by King Louis XVI to Versailles. The American met author and philosopher François-Marie Arouet de Voltaire at the Académie des Sciences, where he soon became a member. Through such associations, he made himself more than just a begging diplomat looking for alms from the French in the way of ships, troops, and war loans. Through his energetic self-promotion and outreach to both high- and low-born French, he soon morphed into a pop-culture celebrity, and a man to whom it was very hard to say "no."

HENRY LAURENS'S ORDEAL

Franklin's fellow peace commissioner Henry Laurens—a Carolina planter who had once been president of the Continental Congress—saw his fate mixed with that of Cornwallis in an odd and disturbing way.

During 1780, while aboard a ship bound from Philadelphia to Holland (where he hoped to negotiate a $10-million loan from the Dutch), Laurens found himself captured by the British. He then spent 15 months imprisoned in the Tower of London. Under the harsh conditions, his health deteriorated. To add insult to injury, the patriot was forced by his British hosts to pay "room and board"—and even to pay the wages of his guards.

A portrait of Laurens hangs today in the United States Capitol Building. This painting depicts the statesman as he appeared in 1781 during his time in the Tower. Inscribed in the upper left corner of the canvas are the words "Hon: Henry Laurens, Pres. of the American Congress. (Painted 1781, while in the Tower.)" In the painting, Laurens looks away. In his left hand he holds a letter. A red curtain hangs behind him, behind which is a view of

In 1779, the Continental Congress sent Henry Laurens to Holland in the hopes of obtaining a $10-million loan from the Dutch. Unfortunately, while in route, Laurens was captured by the British and forced to spend the next 15 months in the Tower of London.

a building resembling the Tower. Laurens's face bears a dignified and deeply serious look. This portrait was in fact painted during Laurens's time in the Tower. Laurens actually posed in his own cell. The letter that he holds bears the following words: "I have

HENRY LAURENS
(1724-1792)

Reluctant Revolutionary

Born in Charleston, South Carolina, in 1724, Henry Laurens was the son of a well-to-do saddle manufacturer. During 1744, his father sent him to England to study, but he was forced to return to Charleston in 1747 following his father's death. Through the following years, Laurens did very well as a merchant. He imported products such as rum from the West Indies. He also brought in manufactured goods from England. As an exporter, Laurens dealt in products of the American South. These included rice, tar, pitch, deerskins, Carolina indigo, and lumber. Laurens was a shrewd investor, and put most of his profits into land investments throughout South Carolina and Georgia. Thus, by the time of the revolution, Laurens was a fabulously wealthy man.

Regarding the revolution, Laurens was at the same time committed and sad. His sadness had its roots in sentimentality for the land he referred to more than once as "Mother England." Shortly after the signing of the Declaration of Independence, Laurens wrote that he regretted the separation between America and England, despite the fact that he thought it necessary. "Even at this moment I feel a Tear of affection for the good Old Country & for the People in it whom in general I dearly love."

Laurens held a seat in the first South Carolina Provincial Congress. He also served as president of the South Carolina Council of Safety. He likewise served on the 1776 committee charged to draft the state's first constitution, and became vice president of the state

acted the part of a fait[hful] / subject. I now go resolved still to labour for / peace at the same time determined in the / last event to stand or fall with my country./ I have the honour to be / Henry Laurens."

under that new constitution. On the national front, Laurens went to the Continental Congress in 1777 as a representative from South Carolina, and in November of that year was elected president of the Congress. As president, Laurens played a leading role in the establishment of the French Alliance and helped to craft the Articles of Confederation.

Laurens was a close personal friend of fellow southerner General George Washington. He was also one of Washington's firmest supporters. While Washington led the American Army, Laurens saw to it that Congress gave Washington all the support, power, and authority he needed in order to do his job and bring victory against the British forces.

Laurens resigned the presidency of the Continental Congress on December 9, 1778, and soon journeyed to Europe. He returned to America in 1784, following his time in the Tower of London and his work in helping to negotiate the Treaty of Paris. After his return, Laurens retired from public life. As an old man, he focused entirely on his family and his businesses—which included, as the years progressed, an involvement with the slave trade, which he personally professed to hate. As a private citizen building business ties across the Atlantic, Laurens thereafter always did his personal best to heal and improve relations between the former colonies and Great Britain, which he always continued to view as the motherland. To the end of his life, Laurens saw the former colonies as heirs to British culture and values. Henry Laurens died in 1792 at the age of 68.

But Laurens had the last laugh. The so-called constable of the Tower was none other than Lord Charles Cornwallis himself, the British commander whose embarrassing surrender to George Washington at Yorktown essentially decided the outcome of the American Revolution in favor of the rebels. Laurens was eventually freed by the crestfallen constable. He thereafter journeyed to Paris, where he would aid in the final rounds of peace negotiations.

THE TEMPESTUOUS ARTHUR LEE

Arthur Lee—heir of the prominent Virginia family that would one day produce Confederate general Robert E. Lee—argued with and defamed not only Franklin, but also fellow diplomat Silas Deane of Connecticut. Congress sent Deane to Paris during the early months of 1776. His assigned task was to open trade relations with the French, buy powder and guns for the American Army, and work to make the French government recognize American independence. He met with success early on, in large measure due to the fact that the French already felt anger toward Great Britain and British interests. Present for generations in French culture, this sentiment had recently been sharpened to a fine point by French losses in the Seven Years' War against Great Britain. Thus, even before the 1777 Battle of Saratoga—the first major American victory, and the first event to hint at hope for the revolution's success—France (then officially still neutral) had already, quietly and without fanfare, begun sending needed supplies at Deane's request.

In fact, Deane did just fine in Paris until Benjamin Franklin and Arthur Lee arrived on the scene as fellow commissioners to negotiate a treaty of cooperation and commerce with France. Although Franklin and Deane got along well, there was, from the very start, significant friction, disagreement, and jealousy between Deane and Lee. In time, Lee completely broke from Franklin and Deane (both of whom he suspected of disloyalty) and began sending word of his unhappiness and disagreements to his prominent family back in America. As a result, Congress recalled Silas Deane in late 1778, initially criticizing and casting suspicion on his eager recruitment of French officers for George Washington's army. Later, the Lees and their cohorts accused Deane of being corrupt. Deane struck back with interviews and letters in the press through which he and his friends vigorously argued that the charge was false. No one came out looking good. Lee earned a reputation as someone who fired up scandals. The tarnished Deane wound up spending the rest of his life in exile.

Perhaps Lee had been jealous of Deane because Deane found success in his diplomatic errand in France, and Lee had found only failure when dispatched on a similar errand to Spain. Early in 1777, Lee went to Spain as American commissioner, but received a cold welcome. He was not even allowed to enter the capital city of Madrid, but instead was packed off to the town of Burgos. And he was not recognized as the representative of a valid government. Until the appointment of Jay, however, Lee continued to at least act as commissioner to Spain, and eventually achieved one very small result. During January 1778, he was able to obtain the promise of a loan of 3,000,000 livres, only a fraction of which (some 170,000 livres) was ever paid.

During June 1779, Lee went to Berlin (then the capital of Prussia), where—once again—he did not enjoy officially recognized status. Eventually he cosigned with Franklin and Deane the treaties of cooperation and commerce between America and France in February 1778, even though he had virtually nothing to do with the negotiation of these agreements. An unsympathetic character, Lee made himself generally unpopular throughout elite circles in France, Spain, and Prussia. Receiving a recall notice from Congress in late 1779, he returned to America in September 1780, much to Franklin's delight.

In 1781, Lee became a member of the Virginia House of Delegates; after that he served in the Continental Congress from 1782 through 1785. Along with Oliver Wolcott and Richard Butler, he arranged a key treaty with the Six Nations of the Iroquois Confederacy during 1784. Later, in partnership with George Clark and Richard Butler, he arranged a similar treaty with the Wyandot, Delaware, Chippewa, and Ottawa Indians, signed in January 1785. Lee died at his plantation at Urbana, Virginia, on December 12, 1792.

JOHN JAY ARRIVES IN PARIS

John Jay arrived in Paris from Madrid in late June 1782. Shortly after that, he made a lengthy report by letter to Robert R. Livingston, president of the Continental Congress:

> My letters from Madrid, and afterwards a few lines from Bordeaux, informed you of my being called to this place by a pressing letter from Dr. Franklin. . . . After placing my family in a hotel, I immediately went out to Passy, and spent the remainder of the afternoon in conversing with Dr. Franklin on the subjects which had induced him to write to me. I found that he had then more reason to think my presence necessary than it seems to be at present. Yesterday we paid a visit to Count de Vergennes. He gave me a very friendly reception, and entered pretty fully with us into the state of the negotiation. His answer to the British Minister appeared to me ably drawn. It breathes great moderation, and yet is so general as to leave room for such demands as circumstances, at the time of the treaty, may render convenient.
>
> There is reason to believe that Mr. Fox and Lord Shelburne are not perfectly united, and that [Caesar] Rodney's success will repress the ardour of our enemies for an immediate peace. . . . Mr. Adams cannot leave Amsterdam at present, and I hear that Mr. Laurens thinks of returning soon to America, so that I apprehend Dr. Franklin and myself will

John Jay was elected president of the Continental Congress in 1778 and later served as a minister to both France and Spain. In May 1782, Jay joined Benjamin Franklin in Paris to serve as joint negotiator in peace talks with Great Britain.

be left to manage at least the skirmishing business, if I may so call it, of our commission, without the benefit of their counsel and assistance. You know what I think and feel on this subject, and I wish things were so circumstanced as to admit of my being indulged. . . . I shall endeavor to get lodgings as near to Dr. Franklin as I can. He is in perfect good health, and his mind appears more vigorous than that of any man of his age I have known. He certainly is a valuable Minister, and an agreeable companion.

JOHN JAY
(1745–1829)

New York Federalist

John Jay, noted both as an American statesman and as the first chief justice of the United States Supreme Court, was born in New York City in 1745.

Jay graduated from King's College (now Columbia University) in 1764, and earned the right to practice law in 1768. Eventually he became a partner of Robert R. Livingston, heir of the incredibly wealthy Hudson Valley family. Jay's marriage to Sarah Livingston, a daughter of William Livingston, assured his social prominence and wealth going forward.

Before the American Revolution, Jay argued against a formal break with Great Britain while he at the same time criticized London's colonial policies. Once the revolution began, however, Jay became a passionate and uncompromising patriot who vowed he would not rest until British troops had been driven from American soil.

Jay served as a delegate to the First and Second Continental congresses, and also worked as a member of the Provincial Congress of New York throughout 1777. In the latter body, he played an important role in orchestrating the first draft of the New York State Constitution. Toward the close of 1777, Jay himself was drafted to serve as the first chief justice for the Supreme Court of the State of New York. It was a post he held until December 1778, when he left to take up the position of president of the Continental Congress. The year 1779 saw Jay traveling to Spain as ambassador.

A few days later, on June 28, Jay wrote again to Livingston, this time to warn against commissioners rumored to have been dispatched to the American mainland by the king and

Following his work with Franklin and Adams on the Treaty of Paris, Jay refused any further diplomatic appointments. Returning home, he accepted Congress's appointment as secretary of Foreign Affairs under the Articles of Confederation. He held this post from 1784 through 1789, at which point the adoption of the new U.S. Constitution made the job obsolete.

Jay is most noted for his contributions to the Federalist movement, headed by Alexander Hamilton, which argued for a strong central government and a leadership structure dominated by wealthy men and families.

Importantly, he also became the first chief justice of the U.S. Supreme Court, serving from 1789 through 1795. In this capacity, he crafted early decisions of the Court that played key roles in defining and helping shape the new government of the United States. During his time as chief justice, Jay played out one final diplomatic mission. When issues left unaddressed by the Treaty of Paris threatened to revive hostilities between the United States and Great Britain, Jay went to England in 1794 and concluded what is today known as Jay's Treaty. This agreement ensured that the British would abandon forts in the American Northwest and addressed various other issues of commerce and navigation.

Following this, Jay ran unsuccessfully for the governorship of New York in 1792, when he lost to George Clinton. He ran again in 1795, however, this time winning. He was reelected, and served until 1801. Thereafter, he retired to his farm at Bedford in New York's Hudson Valley, where he died in 1829.

Parliament. "The intentions of the British Ministry with respect to us are by no means clear," he noted, and continued:

> They [the British] are divided upon the subject. It is said that Mr. Fox and his friends incline to meet us on the terms of independence, but that Lord Shelburne and his adherents entertain an idea of making a compact with us, similar to that between Britain and Ireland, and there is room to apprehend that efforts will be made to open a negotiation on these subjects at Philadelphia. When it is considered that the articles of a general peace cannot be discussed in America, and that propositions for a separate one ought not to be listened to, it is evident to me that their sending out commissions can be calculated for no other purpose than that of intrigue.
>
> I should enlarge on this topic, were I not persuaded that you will see this matter in the same point of view, and that any proposition which they may offer will be referred to the American Commissioners in Europe. How far it may be prudent to permit any British agents to come into our country, on such an ostensible errand, is an easy question, for where an unnecessary measure may be dangerous it should be avoided. They may write from New York whatever they may have to propose, and may receive answers in the same manner.
>
> If one may judge from appearances, the Ministry are very desirous of getting some of their emissaries into our country, either in an avowed or in a private character, and, all things considered, I should think it most safe not to admit any Englishman in either character within our lines at this very critical juncture. A mild and yet firm resolution, on the impropriety and inexpediency of any negotiation for peace in America, would give great satisfaction to our friends and confirm their confidence in us. We, indeed, who know our country, would apprehend no danger from any thing that

British agents might say or do to deceive or divide us; but the opinions of strangers, who must judge by appearances, merit attention; and it is doubtless best not only to be steadfast to our engagements, but also to avoid giving occasion to the slightest suspicions of a contrary disposition. An opinion does prevail here, that in the mass of our people there is a considerable number who, though resolved on independence, would nevertheless prefer an alliance with England to one with France, and this opinion will continue to have a certain degree of influence during the war. This circumstance renders much circumspection necessary.

Proper Means

Ironically, Benjamin Franklin had as many social contacts in Great Britain as he had in France. Franklin—who had spent some 17 years living in Great Britain before the American Revolution—had many friends there and kept up those friendships via correspondence throughout the period of hostilities. Franklin regularly exchanged letters with British statesman Edmund Burke, diplomat David Hartley, and others. He also maintained his membership in the Royal Society (Great Britain's most important scientific organization) and still submitted the occasional article to the society's journal. During the summer of 1782, he took time out from the peace negotiations to write the following to the Royal Society's president:

> Be assured that I long earnestly for a return of those peaceful times when I could sit down in sweet society with my English

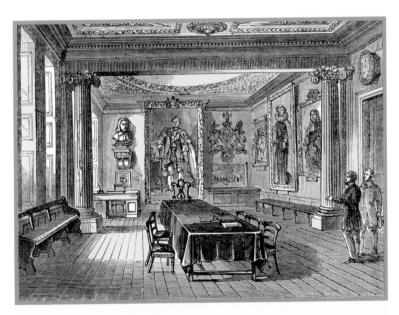

Benjamin Franklin was a member of the prestigious Royal Society of London (depicted here), which was established in 1660 by Sir Christopher Wren. The organization is the oldest national scientific society in the world and promotes scientific research in Great Britain.

philosophical friends. Much more happy should I be thus employed in your most desirable company than in that of all the grandees [noblemen] of the earth projects plans of mischief, however necessary they may be supposed for obtaining greater good. . . . If proper means are used to produce, not only a peace, but what is much more interesting, a thorough reconciliation, a few years may heal the wounds that have been made in our happiness, and produce a degree of prosperity of which at present we can hardly form a conception.

To another British friend, he added:

America and her mother land can never be truly parted. Financially and politically, yes—*but not spiritually*. The child leaves the home, the young bird leaves the nest, and the next phase begins. But ancestral ties endure, the child looks back fondly, and old debts are remembered and made good. I would foresee more than one Anglo-American alliance in our combined futures, we who rise from the same roots, we whose ancient fathers for millennium lie in the same ground. We share language and history and literature. We share the Enlightenment. We share common dreads, as well as common obligations to that which is God. Where shall we go from here? Who can guess? But I daresay we are bound to travel together.

Benjamin Franklin ultimately was an idealist who sought peace and cooperation among all Western powers. He earnestly believed that such a thing should and could be possible. Some of his peers in diplomacy—including the British and French and even his fellow Americans—believed him to be naïve. But these peers missed a major point about Franklin: He only sounded naïve in his letters and in his backstage, off-the-record conversations with fellow Americans such as Adams and Jay. Adams and Jay took him seriously and, as a result, came away alarmed. In the real arena of politics, Franklin was considerably less innocent than otherwise advertised. At the bargaining table, he was absolutely not a diplomatic pushover.

NEGOTIATIONS PROCEED

Several weeks passed before the Earl of Shelburne's views—the pursuit of a genuine peace among all parties—prevailed in the British cabinet. After this, the colonial secretary's victory was quickly sealed by an event beyond anyone's control. Lord Rockingham died July 1 of that year, and King George III selected Shelburne as the next prime minister. Both Fox and Grenville resigned their positions. Shelburne then appointed the agreeable Thomas Robinson, the first Baron Grantham, as foreign secretary. Grantham in turn appointed Alleyne Fitzherbert to negotiate with Charles de Vergennes toward a genuine peace, while Richard Oswald continued his talks with Franklin.

Franklin had shrugged off Fox's previous proposals, despite the promise of fast and easy independence for the former colonies. He also retained the confidence of Shelburne, with whom he shared a similar political philosophy. In this atmosphere, as both a representative of the Continental Congress and a friend, Franklin was able to convince Shelburne that Americans would simply not settle for anything less than total and complete independence. At the same time, however, Franklin made clear that once Great Britain recognized America as a sovereign power, America would exert every effort to assist the British in achieving a peace with the other involved nations.

Early in the summer, Oswald showed Franklin a memorandum from Shelburne. In it the new prime minister mentioned obtaining "a final settlement of things between Great Britain and America, which Dr. Franklin very properly says requires to be treated in a very different manner from the peace between Great Britain and France, who have always been at enmity with each other." Shelburne had two motives in writing this letter. First, he wanted Franklin to let him know the Americans' terms so that talks could move forward. Second, Shelburne wanted Fitzherbert's negotiations with Vergennes to move quickly. He wished for the signing of Great Britain's treaty with America to fit in with the signing of similar documents with France.

In a subsequent and secret memo to Oswald, Franklin laid out "necessary" provisions for a peace, as well as "advisable" ones. The four "necessary" and therefore nonnegotiable items included "full and complete" independence for America, removal of all British troops, secured borders, and fishing rights off the Canadian coast. "Advisable" conditions included monetary payments to compensate for the destruction inflicted by British forces during the war, acknowledgement of British guilt for the war, a free trade agreement, and that the British give up Canada to the United States.

The EARL of SHELBURNE.

In July 1782, the Earl of Shelburne became British prime minister when Lord Rockingham died. Shelburne was an old friend of Benjamin Franklin and was a key figure in convincing the British government to recognize American sovereignty.

Of course, Franklin only inserted these "advisable" conditions to distract the British from the more important issues. This gave the British something to reject, and therefore feel they had some power in the negotiations. By comparison, all his "necessary" proposals seemed more than acceptable. That July, before Adams arrived in Paris, and while Jay lay in bed with influenza, Franklin put the essentials of an Anglo-American agreement in place. Before the summer was out, Shelburne accepted the concept of total American independence. He also promised to grant generous peace terms related to some side issues, such as territorial boundaries. Shelburne informed Oswald that Franklin's written proposal provided "unequivocal proofs of Dr. Franklin's sincerity." So long as the Americans would drop the "advisable" provisions, and keep only "those called necessary . . . as the ground of discussion," then he was sure that a treaty could be "speedily concluded." He would also comply with Franklin's demand that American independence be formally recognized before real official negotiations began in earnest. Franklin wanted to ensure that no one would mistake independence for one of the debatable items.

"Our British counterparts are poised for surrender, so long as we take pains not to make it look as such," Franklin wrote a colleague back home. "We are in sight of port, and we hope no storm cloud will suddenly loom up over the horizon. I endeavor to keep our French friends calm and satisfied, and believe I do so. I remain intrigued, as always, by the future, with all its complications and all its likely successes and disappointments."

FRANKLIN'S STRENGTHENING POSITION

Throughout the summer of 1782 Franklin's hand in negotiations was strengthened in several subtle ways, and he knew it.

First, Vergennes had softened on the question of separate negotiations. Now, suddenly, Vergennes saw direct and separate talks between France and Great Britain as highly desirable: the fastest likely route to a treaty. Why Vergennes's sudden willingness? The real answer lay on the Black Sea. Russia's Catherine the Great was showing interest in gobbling up the Crimea, a region now part of Ukraine, located on the shores of the Black Sea in eastern Europe. Vergennes and all of France wished to block Russia's territorial expansion, but would need Great Britain's help in doing so. And of course, any British and French cooperation on the Black Sea would be impossible so long as the two powers remained at war. On the other side of the negotiations, Richard Oswald admitted to Franklin the serious financial problems that the British had fallen into during the course of the war. "Our enemies may now do what they please with us," he confided. "They have the ball at their foot."

Given these realities, Franklin increased his demands over what they had been in the spring. Previously, in informal conversations with Oswald, he had been purposely vague on the boundaries of Canada and suggested that he would consider the idea of using the proceeds from the sale of Canadian land to compensate British sympathizers for properties confiscated by the Continental Congress. Now, however, Franklin voiced a firm argument indicating that Canada did not, and would never, stretch south of the Great Lakes. (As a bonus, this line of reasoning implied that the western boundary of the new United States reached to the Mississippi River, effectively removing that border from discussion and debate.) Franklin now offered absolutely nothing to British sympathizers in the way of compensation. Instead, he gave a vague statement that the commissioners might eventually recommend compensation.

"There is no need," Franklin wrote home in a confidential note, "for us to give more than just a little, if that, to secure peace on our terms. All parties seem wounded, we the least. All parties seem anxious, we the least. The new world appears to triumph in some ways over the old. The new world seems the

After the Earl of Shelburne became British prime minister, he appointed Richard Oswald peace commissioner in Paris. Franklin and Oswald (depicted here) spent a great deal of time hammering out the terms of the Treaty of Paris.

safest right now. The French and British dread the Russians. The British dread the French and Spanish and Dutch. And so forth. Only we Americans, protected by the luxury of the Atlantic, seem secure on all points."

JOHN JAY, OUT OF THE ACTION

While all this went on, Jay slowly recovered in his Paris hotel. Franklin visited him regularly and, standing at a safe distance, told him what was going on in the negotiations, while Jay, barely able to speak and weak with fever, nodded dumbly. By mid-July, he was able to take short carriage rides up toward Passy, where Franklin lived on a pleasant hill overlooking the Seine River, adjoining the beautiful park, Bois de Boulogne. Jay's physician brother, Dr. James Jay, carefully monitored his progress and saw to his needs. (This same Dr. Jay invented the invisible ink used by General George Washington for secret communications.) "John had worried he would disappear into death," James Jay wrote home that summer. He continued:

> ... but now he appears to slowly mend. The breathing is easier, the fevers less frequent, the promise of tomorrow brighter. I know him anxious to be taking part in the great talks ongoing. I know him to be concerned that terms be as he would have them be. While respectful of Dr. Franklin, he implies a certain hesitancy that stands in the way of complete faith. Perhaps that master of lightning bolts is no master of ambassadors? I do not pretend to know; my brother does pretend to know, more than pretend, and has his doubts. We are both concerned, of course, about the dominance of the French in the talks general, and on Dr. Franklin's mental horizon. Perhaps we are oversensitive on this issue, being of Huguenot stock and blessed—damned?—with long ancestral memories.

The memories James Jay referred to were this: The Protestant French Huguenots were members of the Reformed Church, established by John Calvin in 1550. Although the source of the name *Huguenot* remains unclear, it appears to date from about 1550, when it shows up in records of court cases against "heretics" charged with breaking the rules of the Roman Catholic Church. In January 1536, a general proclamation of the French king, supported by the Roman Catholic Church, actually called for the outright extermination of all Huguenots. During the spring of 1562, no fewer than 1,200 Huguenots were murdered at Vassy, France. This massacre triggered the so-called Wars of Religion, which dominated French society and history for the next 30 years. During the summer of 1572, more than 8,000 Parisian Huguenots met their end in the infamous St. Bartholomew Massacre. Even after the Wars of Religion, French persecution of the Huguenots continued. Murders and massacres were common. Partial rights for Huguenots were enacted with a new declaration on November 28, 1787—but even then they were not treated as equals in French society. Thus the Jays, given their ancestry, had reason to view France—and the French people in general—with suspicion.

The fact that John Jay survived his brother's "medical treatments" is almost as miraculous as the French Huguenots surviving years of persecution. James Jay used the most popular treatments of the time. These included potentially lethal doses of mercury, which would in theory kill the influenza virus if they did not kill the patient first. (As an example, during this same era, the composer Mozart died of mercury toxicity during a course of treatment for syphilis.) James also "bled" his brother and applied leaches. Perhaps because of these remedies, John approached death's door not once but three times before finally rallying for good, and displaying enough internal recovery power to be spared further "cures."

"John seems better," James wrote in mid-July,

His fevers and chills are passed, and his shaking suspended. Exhaustion seems the main thing now—exhaustion after the grueling fight for survival. But each day his weakened body seems a small bit stronger. Each day he appears closer to his old self. He takes new interest in the papers, and in Dr. Franklin's reports in deceits. The good Mr. Franklin finds him a bit more declarative, suspicious and questioning than before and—I think—may have liked him much better layed [sic] down with the fever between the sheets. John has been revived as an animal of debate and argument, albeit somewhat breathlessly stated with eyes closed half the time.

Methinks he will put his own mark on these proceedings very shortly, and that it will be a good departure. I am no man of these affairs myself, but I can tell Dr. Franklin is too at home with those whom he presumes to negotiate with. He is everyone's friend and everyone's ally, and always talks grandly of "mankind" along with the "brotherhood of nations." John grimaces at these phrases. He thinks them unhelpful in satisfying American wants and needs. He also believes that a fair amount of healthy suspicion pointed in the direction of London, Versailles, Madrid and elsewhere is called for, whereas Dr. Franklin seems less so disposed. When John finally emerges and walks among the living—a moment that will come quite soon—the permutations promise to be fascinating.

While he was sick that July, Jay received greetings from Adams, still delayed in the Netherlands. "I shall beg the favor of you to write me from time to time the progress of the negotiations for peace," Adams wrote. "I hope in God that your Spanish negotiation has not wrecked your constitution as my Dutch one has mine. I would not undergo again what I have suffered in body and mind for the fee simple of all their Spice Islands. I love them, however, because with all their faults and under all their disadvantages they have at bottom a strong spirit of Liberty, a sincere affection for America and a kind of religious veneration for her cause."

But Adams—like Jay—believed America's allies must be watched to make sure they did not plot to form a peace more in their interest than in that of the former colonies. "There are intrigues going on here, which originate in Petersburg and Copenhagen which surprise me," he wrote. He continued:

> They succeed very ill, but they are curious. Have you discerned any coming from the same sources at Madrid or Versailles? Whether the object of them is to stir up a party in favor of England to take a part in the war or only to favor her in obtaining moderate terms of peace, or whether it is simply to share some of her guineas by an amusement of this kind, like a game of cards, is a problem. As to peace, no party in England seems to have influence enough to dare to make one real advance towards it. The present Ministers are really to be pitied. They have not power to do any thing. I am surprised they don't all resign; if they dissolve Parliament I don't believe they would get a better one.

Jay in
Ascendance

John Jay's rally to good health was especially well timed, as it came at the same time that a round of bad health suddenly rose from the gut of Franklin. Just as Jay emerged from his bed, Franklin took to his own pillows. The old man had long suffered from gout, a painful swelling of the joints often partially caused by drinking large amounts of alcohol and eating fatty foods. Now the same lifestyle that had produced the gout yielded yet another penalty. Kidney stones bloodied Franklin's urine and doubled him over in pain. The sickness afflicted Franklin through much of August and into September. Thus he was forced to leave some weeks of negotiation to Jay, and then eventually to Jay in collaboration with Adams. Franklin enjoyed a few good days in the months of August and September, when he was able to get out to speak with Vergennes and/or Oswald. But for the bulk of this period, John Jay ruled the negotiations.

On August 2, shortly after taking up the reins of the negotiation, Jay wrote to Adams to keep him informed of progress:

> Your negotiations in Holland have been honourable to yourself as well as useful to your country. I rejoice in both, and regret that your health has been so severely taxed by the business of your employers. I have also had my share of perplexities, and some that I ought not to have met with. I congratulate you on the prospect of your loan succeeding, and hope that your expectations on that subject may be realized. I commend your prudence, however, in not relying on appearances. They deceive us sometimes in all countries. . . . [I] hope that when your business at the Hague will admit of a few weeks' absence you may prevail upon yourself to pay us a visit. I really think that a free conference between us might be useful as well as agreeable, especially as we should thereby have an opportunity of making many communications to each other that must not be communicated on paper.
>
> As to negotiations for peace, they have been retarded by the late changes in the British Ministry. Mr. Oswald is here, and I hear that Mr. Fitzherbert is to succeed Mr. Grenville. Lord Shelburne continues to profess a desire for peace, but his professions, unless supported by acts, can have little credit with us. He says that our independence shall be acknowledged, but it is not done, and therefore his sincerity remains questionable. War must make peace for us, and we shall always find well appointed armies to be our ablest negotiators.

JAY'S FIRST ROUND WITH THE BRITISH

As indicated in his letter to Adams, the first action Jay took was to argue with the wording of Oswald's Parliamentary and Royal Commission to negotiate. Both Oswald and Shelburne assured Franklin that American independence would be set prior to the final negotiations. But even so, no one in England had taken the time to put this assurance in writing. Thus Jay—perhaps simply to stake his territory, and put all parties on notice that he intended to be a stickler for detail—formally took issue with the wording of the Brits' commission. That document authorized Oswald to negotiate "with the said colonies and plantations" rather than with an independent republic, the United States of America. Jay demanded that that change be made before the talks proceeded further.

Franklin saw this demand as an unnecessary and useless delay. "Liberty lurks not in the fine print of commissions, but in the treaty itself," he mumbled in a note to his grandson. Elsewhere, he added, "Jay insists on winning the battle at the risk of losing the war. The British will take only so much in the way of insult." In this spirit, Franklin dragged Jay to visit Vergennes's office in the Palace of Versailles. Franklin's hope was that Vergennes would be able to talk Jay out of his position. To Franklin's delight, Vergennes declared that it did not seem necessary to him to insist that Oswald's commission contain a clear declaration of American sovereignty. At this, Franklin echoed his own opinion that Oswald's written instructions and authorization "would do" as they stood. Writing home after the meeting, Franklin said he interpreted Vergennes's comment as further proof of the Frenchman's approval for the British-American negotiations to proceed. It was a generous and supportive gesture that displayed the French Crown's "gracious good will."

Jay interpreted Vergennes's remark in a more sinister—and, perhaps, more realistic—manner. Jay guessed, correctly, that Vergennes did not want Great Britain to recognize American independence except as part of a wide-ranging peace settlement that also addressed concerns and settled accounts with France and Spain. "This [French] Court chooses to postpone an acknowledgement of our independence by Britain," Jay

Foreign Minister Charles Gravier, count de Vergennes, was France's chief representative during the negotiations between Great Britain, France, and the United States leading up to the signing of the Treaty of Paris. Vergennes supported American sovereignty but only if France's concerns were also addressed.

reported to Congress, "in order to keep us under their direction until not only their and our objects are attained, but also until Spain shall be gratified in her demands. . . . I ought to add that Dr. Franklin does not see the conduct of this Court in the light [that] I do, and that he believes they mean nothing in their proceedings but what is friendly, fair and honourable."

In a letter to Robert Livingston, Jay provided complete details of the meeting with Vergennes:

> On the 10th of August we waited upon the Count de Vergennes, and a conference between him and us on the subject of Mr. Oswald's commission ensued. The Count declared his opinion that we might proceed to treat with Mr. Oswald under it as soon as the original should arrive. He said it was such a one as we might have expected it would be, but that we must take care to insert proper articles in the treaty, to secure our independence and our limits against all future claims. I observed to the Count that it would be descending from the ground of independence to treat under the description of Colonies. He replied, that names signified little; that the King of Great Britain's styling himself the King of France was no obstacle to the King of France's treating with him; that an acknowledgment of our independence, instead of preceding, must in the natural course of things be the effect of the treaty, and that it would not be reasonable to expect the effect before the cause. He added, that we must be mindful to exchange powers with Mr. Oswald, for that his acceptance of our powers, in which we were styled Commissioners from the United States of America, would be a tacit admittance of our independence. I made but little reply to all this singular reasoning. The Count turned to Dr. Franklin and asked him what he thought of the matter. The Doctor said he believed the commission would do. He next asked my opinion. I told him that I did not like it, and that it was best to proceed cautiously.

To this information, Jay added information concerning Franklin's opinion:

> On returning, I could not forbear observing to Dr. Franklin that it was evident the Count did not wish to see our independence acknowledged by Britain until they had made all their uses of us. It was easy for them to foresee difficulties in bringing Spain into a peace on moderate terms, and that if we once found ourselves standing on our own legs, our independence acknowledged, and all our other terms ready to be granted, we might not think it our duty to continue in the war for the attainment of Spanish objects. But, on the contrary, as we were bound by treaty to continue the war till our independence should be attained, it was the interest of France to postpone that event until their own views and those of Spain could be gratified by a peace, and that I could not otherwise account for the Minister's advising us to act in a manner inconsistent with our dignity, and for reasons which he himself had too much understanding not to see the fallacy of. The Doctor imputed this conduct to the moderation of the Minister, and to his desire of removing every obstacle to speedy negotiations for peace. He observed that this Court had hitherto treated us very fairly, and that suspicions to their disadvantage should not be readily entertained. He also mentioned our instructions, as further reasons for our acquiescence in the advice and opinion of the Minister. A day or two afterward I paid a visit to Mr. Oswald, and had a long conversation with him respecting his commission.

Writing to Franklin several months earlier—in March 1782—Jay had insisted that French and American interests remained bound together, but that Spanish and Dutch interests need not be a part of the equation for a peace treaty involving the Americans and the British. He wrote:

conduct if we are betrayed into negotiations, in or out of a congress, before this point is settled; if gold and diamonds, and every insidious intrigue and wicked falsehood can induce anybody to embarrass us, and betray us into truces

JOHN ADAMS
(1735–1826)

Stern New Englander

John Adams served as the second president of the United States (1797–1801). He was born in Quincy, Massachusetts, in 1735, and graduated from Harvard College in 1755. His son John Quincy Adams also served as president.

As a young Boston attorney, Adams was stiff, abrasive, and frighteningly eloquent. He went on to serve in both the First and Second Continental congresses, where he took the initiative to nominate George Washington for the position of commander of the Continental troops in the war against the British. Along with Benjamin Franklin and Thomas Jefferson, Adams played an important role in the congressional committee empowered to draft the Declaration of Independence.

Following the Treaty of Paris, Adams served from 1785 through 1788 as American minister to Great Britain. In that position, he dealt almost daily with British haughtiness and outright refusal to deal with ongoing problems left unaddressed by the Treaty of Paris (items later addressed in Jay's Treaty). Frustrated by this, Adams finally requested his own recall.

Once back in the United States, Adams found himself drafted as the nation's first vice president. He served throughout George Washington's administration (1789–1797). In the 1796 election, voters chose Adams to succeed Washington as president.

Adams's administration was, like Adams himself, complex. As president, Adams stood by his unbending, unblinking integrity.

and bad conditions, we may depend upon having them played off against us. We are and have been no match for them at this game. We shall have nothing to negotiate with, but integrity, perspicuity and firmness. There is but one way

His general sympathies were with Alexander Hamilton and the Federalists. Adams himself respected the concept of a powerful central government, and a certain limitation of the right to vote, so that democracy would not translate to rule of the masses. Similarly, Adams was suspicious of the Populist Jefferson and his farmer allies. Nevertheless, Adams refused to blindly follow the Federalist line. Though most Federalists despised France, Adams worked vigorously to avoid war with that country as a result of fallout from the notorious XYZ Affair in 1797–98. Similarly, Adams refused to strenuously support the infamous Alien and Sedition Acts of 1798, which were aimed at curbing the free speech of Anti-Federalist politicians and journalists.

Despite Adams's moderation on these issues, he was still disliked by followers of Jefferson. Adams was defeated in the election of 1800, and found himself replaced by none other than Jefferson.

From 1801 onward, Adams lived quietly in Quincy. He would occasionally emerge from the shadow of retirement to write editorials and comment on the issues of the day. However, he spent most of his time enjoying his library and his family. He also began extensive correspondences with colleagues, friends, and thinkers around the globe. Most importantly, near the very end of his life, he began a cordial and important correspondence with his old colleague in revolution and later political adversary, Thomas Jefferson. Ironically, both men died on the same day: Independence Day, July 4, 1826. That date happened to be the fiftieth anniversary of the document they had both signed and helped craft.

to negotiate with Englishmen, that is, clearly and decidedly; their fears only govern them. If we entertain an idea of their generosity or benevolence towards us, we are undone. The pride and vanity of that nation is a disease, it is a delirium, it has been flattered and inflamed so long by themselves and by others that it perverts everything. The moment you depart one iota from your character and the distinct line of sovereignty, they interpret it to spring from fear or love of them, and from a desire to go back.

Taking his point further, Adams added:

Fox saw we were aware of this, and calculated his system accordingly. We must finally come to that idea and so must Britain. The latter will soon come to it if we do not flinch. If we discover the least weakness or wavering, the blood and treasures of our countrymen will suffer for it in a great degree. Firmness! firmness and patience for a few months will carry us triumphantly to that point where it is the interest of our allies, of neutral nations, nay, even of our enemies, that we should arrive. I mean a sovereignty universally acknowledged by all the world; whereas, the least oscillation will, in my opinion, leave us to dispute with the world, and with one another, these fifty years.

To this, Jay responded on September 1 with news of progress. "My opinion coincides with yours as to the impropriety of treating with our enemies on any other than an equal footing," Jay wrote. "We have told Mr. Oswald so, and he has sent an express to London to communicate it and to require further instructions. He has not yet received an answer. Herewith enclosed is a copy of his commission. . . . Mr. Fitzherbert is employed to talk about preliminaries with this Court. Nothing, I think, will be done until the return of Mr. Oswald's express. We shall then be enabled to form some judgment of the British Minister's real intentions."

Nuts and Bolts

John Jay left nothing to chance. After emerging from his meeting with Vergennes and Franklin, he was not only suspicious of the French, but also furious at what he saw to be a conspiracy between the French and the Spanish to the disadvantage of American interests. The Spanish Court had shunned Jay for months, and so he was perhaps especially sensitive when Vergennes brought up the subject of Spain's desire to claim some of the land between the Allegheny Mountains and the Mississippi River. After his meeting with Vergennes, Jay came away more fully convinced than ever that America's so-called allies could easily be persuaded to turn on the new country in return for territory or gold. Jay's suspicions of the French were further aroused in August 1782. He learned then that Vergennes had sent a secret team to London to talk peace in the absence of the Americans.

In response to this, while supposedly "waiting" for an answer to Oswald's call for instructions, Jay sent his own secret messenger to London. The man he sent—without Franklin's knowledge—was Franklin's own longtime friend Benjamin Vaughan, who had recently come to Paris to visit Franklin. Vaughan's instructions were to tell Lord Shelburne directly and clearly that Oswald's commission needed to state that he was to negotiate with "the United States," not the "colonies." Vaughan was to further explain that only a clear acknowledgement of American independence such as this would "cut the cords" binding America to France.

Eager to make a peace before his shaky government toppled, Shelburne soon gave Jay something close to what the American had been lobbying for. During mid-September, Shelburne's cabinet granted Oswald a new commission "to treat with the commissioners appointed by the colonies under the title of 13 united states." At the same meeting, the cabinet reaffirmed that American independence could and should be acknowledged as a preliminary to further discussions. Jay wrote Adams on September 28: "I have only time to inform you that our objections to Mr. Oswald's first commission have produced a second, which arrived yesterday. It empowers him to treat with the Commissioners of the *thirteen United States of America*. I am preparing a longer letter on this subject, but as this intelligence is interesting, I take the earliest opportunity of communicating it."

MOVING WITHOUT FRANCE

In rejecting Vergennes's recommendation, Jay had also gone against instructions from Congress that he and the other commissioners follow the lead of the French in negotiations. For this he made no apologies. Jay explained his actions in an October 15 letter to Gouverneur Morris, the New Yorker who was largely responsible for the final wording of the Constitution. "The king of Great Britain, by letters patent under the great seal, has authorized Mr. Oswald to treat with the commissioners of the *United States of America*," Jay wrote. He continued:

> His first commission literally pursued the Enabling Act, and the authority it gave him was expressed in the very terms of that act, viz., to treat with the colonies, and with any or either of them, and any part of them, and with any description of men in them, and with any person whatsoever, of and concerning peace, etc. *Had I not violated the instructions of Congress* [to follow the French lead in all matters] their dignity would have been in the dust, for the French Minister even took pains not only to persuade us to treat under that commission, but to prevent the second by telling Fitzherbert that the first was sufficient. I told the Minister that we neither could nor would treat with any nation in the world on any other than on an equal footing.

Jay was already confident, and must have felt even more so after he received the following October message from none other than General George Washington: "The changes in the British ministry, and the fluctuation of their councils, are the subjects of universal speculation," Washington wrote. "We wait with impatience to hear the result of the negotiations, and not being very sanguine in our expectations, endeavor to hold ourselves prepared for every contingency. I am certain it will afford you pleasure to know that our army is better organized, disciplined, and clothed, than it has been at any period since the commencement of the war. This you may be assured is the fact."

ADAMS ARRIVES IN PARIS

John Adams arrived in Paris on October 26, 1782. He settled immediately into the Hotel du Roi, bathed in a public bathhouse, consulted a Parisian tailor and wigmaker, and afterward

Shortly after John Jay, John Adams, and Benjamin Franklin began negotiating directly with Great Britain in October 1782, Jay received a letter from General George Washington (depicted here). In the letter, Washington intimated that it was only a matter of time before the British conceded to American demands, which further buoyed Jay's confidence.

stood ready to join Jay and Franklin in the negotiations. From their very first meeting, Adams and Jay got along extremely well. "[Mr. Adams] is very much pleased with Mr. Jay," wrote Adams's friend, the American merchant Matthew Ridley. For his part, Jay commented in his diary that Adams "spoke freely what he thought." On October 28, Jay noted: "Mr. Adams was with me three hours this morning. I mentioned to him the progress and present state of our negotiation with Britain— my conjectures of the views of France and Spain, and the part which it appeared to me advisable for us to act. *He concurred with me in sentiment on all these points.*"

It appears to have been Jay who briefed Adams on Congress's instructions to follow France. Adams immediately joined Jay in objecting to the command. America, Adams insisted, was not fighting a war for independence only to be told what to do by the French. He soon wrote to Robert Livingston to say that he would rather resign than follow such instructions, and that he and Jay were "perfectly agreed" on how the French should be dealt with. He wrote:

> I cannot express it better than in his own words: "to be honest and grateful to our allies, but to think for ourselves."
> I find a construction put upon one article in our instructions by some persons which, I confess, I never put upon it myself. It is represented by some as subjecting us to the French ministry, as taking away from us all right of judging for ourselves, and obliging us to agree to whatever the French ministers should advise us to do, and to do nothing without their consent. I never supposed this to be the intention of Congress. If I had, I never would have accepted the commission, and if I now thought it their intention, I could not continue in it. I cannot think it possible to be the design of Congress. If it is I hereby resign my place in the commission and request that another person may be immediately appointed in my stead.

Of course, it would be months before Adams received an answer from America. In the meantime, he proceeded as though he knew Livingston's answer. Writing about Adams as he appeared in Paris at this time, biographer Walter Isaacson has said:

PREAMBLE AND ARTICLE I OF THE TREATY OF PARIS, 1783

It having pleased the Divine Providence to dispose the hearts of the most serene and most potent Prince George the Third, by the grace of God, king of Great Britain, France, and Ireland, defender of the faith, duke of Brunswick and Lüneburg, arch-treasurer and prince elector of the Holy Roman Empire etc., and of the United States of America, to forget all past misunderstandings and differences that have unhappily interrupted the good correspondence and friendship which they mutually wish to restore, and to establish such a beneficial and satisfactory intercourse, between the two countries upon the ground of reciprocal advantages and mutual convenience as may promote and secure to both perpetual peace and harmony; and having for this desirable end already laid the foundation of peace and reconciliation by the Provisional Articles signed at Paris on the 30th of November 1782, by the commissioners empowered on each part, which articles were agreed to be inserted in and constitute the Treaty of Peace proposed to be concluded between the Crown of Great Britain and the said United States, but which treaty was not to be concluded until terms of peace should be agreed upon between Great Britain and France and his Britannic Majesty should be ready to conclude such treaty accordingly; and the treaty between Great Britain and France having since been concluded, his Britannic Majesty and the United States of America, in order to carry into full effect the Provisional Articles above mentioned, according to the tenor thereof, have constituted and appointed, that is to say his Britannic Majesty on his part, David

Adams was blunt as ever, filled with suspicions and doubting everyone's character but his own. Even Lafayette, who had become Franklin's closest confidant, was immediately slammed by Adams as a "mongrel character" of "unlimited ambition" who was "panting for glory." Adams also

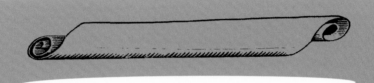

Hartley, Esqr., member of the Parliament of Great Britain, and the said United States on their part, John Adams, Esqr., late a commissioner of the United States of America at the court of Versailles, late delegate in Congress from the state of Massachusetts, and chief justice of the said state, and minister plenipotentiary of the said United States to their high mightinesses the States General of the United Netherlands; Benjamin Franklin, Esqr., late delegate in Congress from the state of Pennsylvania, president of the convention of the said state, and minister plenipotentiary from the United States of America at the court of Versailles; John Jay, Esqr., late president of Congress and chief justice of the state of New York, and minister plenipotentiary from the said United States at the court of Madrid; to be plenipotentiaries for the concluding and signing the present definitive treaty; who after having reciprocally communicated their respective full powers have agreed upon and confirmed the following articles.

Article I:
His Britannic Majesty acknowledges the said United States, viz., New Hampshire, Massachusetts Bay, Rhode Island and Providence Plantations, Connecticut, New York, New Jersey, Pennsylvania, Maryland, Virginia, North Carolina, South Carolina and Georgia, to be free sovereign and independent states, that he treats with them as such, and for himself, his heirs, and successors, relinquishes all claims to the government, propriety, and territorial rights of the same and every part thereof.

Under the Articles of Confederation, Robert Livingston was appointed secretary of the Department of Foreign Affairs, a position he held from 1781 to 1783. Although Livingston did not believe that the American delegates should blindly follow France, he did believe that the French were an integral part of the treaty process.

displayed, in a public and undiplomatic way, his personal distrust of Vergennes by not calling on him for almost three weeks, until the minister "caused him to be reminded of" his duty to do so. [Vergennes, who was as smooth as Adams was rough, baffled the wary Adams by laying on a lavish dinner and plying him with fine wines and Madeira.]

ADAMS AND FRANKLIN

An acre of thin ice lay between Adams and Franklin. The gentleman from Philadelphia had been loudly critical of Adams's diplomatic moves in the past, and they had had other arguments as well. Most recently, Franklin had sent letters to Congress questioning Adams's ability as a commissioner. For several days after first arriving in Paris, Adams put off paying a courtesy call to Franklin at Passy. Finally, when Matthew Ridley insisted that he must, Adams agreed. Then, while putting on his coat to leave, he seemed to change his mind. Ridley recorded in his diary that it was only "with much persuasion [that] I got him at length to go." Writing to his friend Edmund Jennings, Adams elaborated his dislike for Franklin:

> His base jealously of me, and his sordid envy of my commission for making a treaty of commerce with Great Britain have stimulated him to attempt an assassination upon my character at Philadelphia, of which the world has not yet heard, and of which it cannot hear until the time shall come when many voluminous state papers may be laid before the public, which ought not to be until we are all dead. That I have no friendship for Franklin I avow. That I am incapable of having any with a man of his moral sentiments I avow. As far as fate shall compel me to sit with him in public affairs, I shall treat him with decency and perfect impartiality.

To his wife, Abigail, Adams bragged that he and John Jay had together held the line on the point of independence, even though that victory was in fact won before Adams arrived on the scene. He went on to tell her that Franklin—bowing, as usual, to his French friends—"would have taken the advice of the C[omte] de V[ergennes] and treated without, but nobody would join him."

On the day Ridley forced Adams to make his courtesy call on Franklin, Adams stayed with the old man for several hours. As historian David McCullough has written, Adams "seized the opportunity to speak frankly of his opinion of the French Court, as well as to praise Jay for his 'firmness.' Franklin, wrote Adams afterward, 'heard me patiently but said nothing.'" But Franklin soon bowed to the will of his fellow negotiators, which was also—he now had to admit—the will of Congress. Within a week of Adams's arrival in France, Franklin told Jay and Adams: "I am of your opinion and will go on with these [British] gentlemen in the business without consulting this [the French Bourbon] Court." But as the biographer Isaacson has pointed out:

> Franklin's willingness to negotiate without consulting France was not new; he had begun pursuing that approach before Jay and Adams arrived in Paris. But he made it seem that he was doing it partly in deference to the views of his two fellow commissioners, which served to soften Adams's attitude. Franklin "has gone with us in entire harmony and unanimity," Adams happily recorded in his diary, "and has been able and useful, both by his sagacity and his reputation, in the whole negotiation."

Franklin, meanwhile, continued to feel an odd mixture of annoyance mixed with admiration when it came to Adams. Writing to Livingston once the negotiations had concluded, he said of Adams: "He means well for his country, is always an honest man, often a wise one, but sometimes and in some things, absolutely out of his senses."

FORMAL NEGOTIATIONS BEGIN

Although a few formal talks had been held as early as October 5, 1782, between Jay, Franklin, and Oswald, these were delayed for a few weeks after Great Britain succeeded in beating back a joint French–Spanish attack on Gibraltar. In the meantime, Shelburne dispatched cabinet officer Henry Strachey, Shelburne's under-secretary of state, to assist Oswald and—it was rumored—give him some backbone. As we have seen, that same period of time brought Adams's arrival in Paris. With all three of the active American commissioners finally on the same page, and with Shelburne's government having acknowledged American sovereignty, negotiations began in earnest on October 30, which also happened to be Adams's forty-seventh birthday. They would continue through to the last week of November, with Henry Laurens joining his fellow commissioners only in the last few days.

"Starting at eleven each morning," wrote the historian McCullough, "the meetings took place at Jay's lodgings at the Hotel d'Orleans on the Rue des Petits-Augustins on the Left Bank, or at Adams's Hotel du Roi; or the Hotel de Valentinois at Passy, to spare Franklin the ride into Paris in [bad] weather; or at Richard Oswald's quarters at the Grand Hotel Muscovite, also on the Rue des Petits-Augustins." (The weather was indeed bleak. Snow fell over the city nearly every day that November, only to melt in the mild climate as fog engulfed each and every would-be blizzard.)

The weather would prove to be the least of the Brits' problems. It soon became clear that the British envoys were not negotiating at a level that could match that of their American counterparts. The Americans seemed to be far more shrewd, agile, and confident at the bargaining table. Writing in his diary, Adams compared Great Britain to an eagle and America to a cat in an intriguing allegory. The eagle, soaring over a farmer's yard, swept and seized a cat, thinking it to be a rabbit. "In the air the cat seized her by the neck with her teeth and round the body with her fore and hind claws. The eagle finding herself scratched and pressed, bids the cat let go and fall down." But the cat refused, and instead insisted that the eagle fly to the ground and set her down. In the political context, it seemed the British were most anxious to set down the vicious cat America as soon as possible.

Crafting Peace

Benjamin Franklin's grandson William Temple Franklin served as secretary for the Americans. Caleb Whitefoord, meanwhile, served as secretary for Oswald and cabinet officer Strachey. Writing at the time of the proceedings, Whitefoord noted that each of the commissioners "required separate copies of many official Papers, and also Copies [needed to] be made of all papers delivered by them to us. Besides this, Mr. Oswald being of a very active and speculative Mind, was much employed in drawing up Schemes and Plans either on behalf of the Loyalists, and the mother Country, or for annoying our Enemies. Some of those Plans were very long, and [I] generally made two Copies of each; so that [I] had more writing there in one year than [I] ever had in [my] own business in six."

In this manner—with two secretaries, and working five days per week from 11 A.M. until well past supper each

Benjamin Franklin's grandson William Temple Franklin served as secretary for the American delegation at the signing of the Treaty of Paris. After Benjamin Franklin's death in 1790, William Temple became Benjamin's literary heir, publishing much of his grandfather's writings and an autobiography.

evening—the various commissioners worked out complicated matters related to fishing rights off the coast of Newfoundland, prewar debts still owed by Americans to British merchants, the western boundary of the United States along with the question of navigation rights on the Mississippi River, and (finally) the question of compensation for British loyalists in America whose property had been seized.

FISHING RIGHTS

Fishing rights on the Grand Banks off the coast of Newfoundland were a major issue for each of the American commissioners. Fishing in those waters formed a vital industry for men of the Maine, New Hampshire, and Massachusetts coasts. In long rounds of negotiation on this topic, Franklin emphasized that American fishing rights in coastal waters immediately next to those states would eventually benefit Great Britain, too. Profits that Americans made in fishing ventures would undoubtedly be spent to purchase British manufactured goods, the commissioner argued. "Are you afraid," Franklin asked Oswald, "there is not fish enough, or that we should catch too many?"

Adams, however, was the most forceful and eloquent on the issue, speaking poetically about "New England's ancient stake in the sacred codfish." In his own phrase, Adams was "unalterably determined" to agree to nothing that would restrict the rights of New England fishermen. "With the same vitality he had once brought to the courtrooms of Massachusetts and the floor of Congress," wrote McCullough, "[Adams] championed the right of American fishermen, citing articles from treaties past and explaining in details the migratory patterns of the cod, not to say the temperament of seafaring New Englanders, who would refuse to be restrained no matter what the American commissioners proved foolish enough to agree to."

In the end, Oswald agreed to the fishing rights—this to the eventual disappointment of Vergennes, who had secretly hoped to win special fishing rights in those waters for France. But just as the issue seemed settled, Henry Strachey raised one more. Strachey offended Adams by proposing that the line in the treaty specifying the American "right" of fishing should be changed to read "liberty" of fishing. Young Alleyne Fitzherbert seconded Strachey's motion, declaring the word "right" to be "an obnoxious expression." Adams, seething with rage, rose and addressed the British:

Gentlemen, is there or can there be a clearer right? In former treaties, that of Utrecht and that of Paris, France and England have claimed the right and used the word. When God Almighty made the Banks of Newfoundland at 300 leagues distant from the people of America and at 600 leagues distance from those of France and England, did he not give as food a right to the former as to the latter? If Heaven in the Creation have a right, it is ours at least as much as yours. If occupation, use, and possession have a right, we have it as clearly as you. If war and blood and treasure give a right, ours is as good as yours. We have been constantly fighting in Canada, Cape Breton, and Nova Scotia for the defense of the fishery, and have expanded beyond all proportion more than you. If then the right cannot be denied, why then should it not be acknowledged? And put out of dispute?

In the end, the treaty's lines regarding fishing rights wound up reading: "It is agreed that the people of the United States shall continue to enjoy unmolested the right to take fish of every kind on the Grand Bank." But as for the coast of Newfoundland and "all other of his Britannic Majesty's Dominions in America," there American fishermen would have the "liberty" to go about their business. "We did not think," Adams commented many years later, "it necessary to contend for a word."

PREWAR DEBTS

Of the two negotiators on the British side, Strachey came across most forcefully on the matter of the payments of debts owed by Americans to British merchants before the war. Strachey insisted that the treaty must specify that these debts be repaid.

Franklin and Jay answered that neither the commissioners nor Congress could force any of the states to follow that obligation. But then Adams broke in. Adams believed that to say the federal government could not force the states to honor legitimate debts might give an incorrect impression of weakness and incompetence. Worse, it might appear as a confession that no general body of law governed America, and that Congress sat at the mercy of the individual states comprising the union. Besides, said Adams, a debt was a matter of honor. Was America to appear dishonorable?

Later, in private, the three American commissioners gathered together and discussed the issue. Adams pointed out to Jay and Franklin that while it was true Congress could not bind the states to such a provision, it could *recommend* to the states that they open their courts to British creditors seeking the recovery of legitimate debts. Such a statement would satisfy Shelburne by allowing him to appear a hero to his merchants. The next day, the American commissioners made the offer, which was promptly accepted.

THE WESTERN BOUNDARY OF THE UNITED STATES

Franklin cherished a grand vision of American manifest destiny on the continent of North America. He demanded that no other nation have rights to the land between the Alleghenies and the Mississippi River. "He has invariably," wrote Jay, "declared it to be his opinion that we should insist on the Mississippi as our Western boundary." In this, it must be noted, Franklin was at odds with the ambitions of France and Spain. Great Britain, for its part, was fine with allowing the Mississippi to be the western boundary of the new nation, as long as the Crown would have navigation rights, which it would share with America to the exclusion of other powers.

COMPENSATION FOR BRITISH LOYALISTS

The issue of compensation for British Loyalists proved to be the thorniest one of all for the negotiators. Franklin led the arguments against compensation. He argued that the Loyalists had helped cause the war, and that their losses were far less than those suffered by American patriots whose

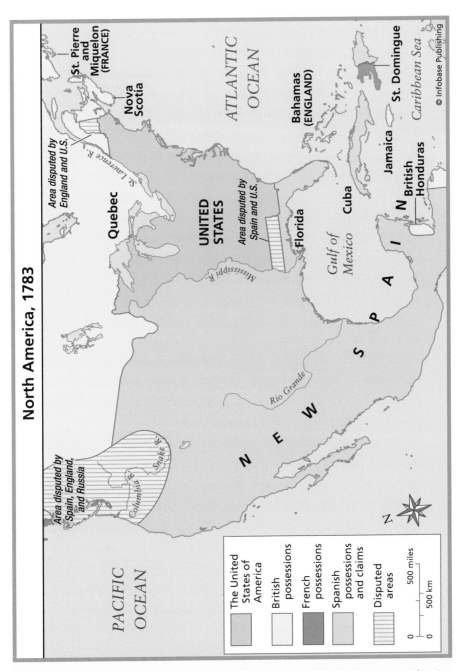

North America, 1783

As this 1783 map of North America illustrates, the United States gained a significant amount of territory from Great Britain as part of the terms of the Treaty of Paris. The new country stretched all the way from the Atlantic seaboard to the Mississippi River.

properties had been taken by the British Redcoats. Franklin's firm stance, although cloaked in the language of politics, was in fact a bitter personal issue for him. Among the Loyalists of whom he spoke was his estranged son William, who was the father of Franklin's secretary and grandson, William Temple Franklin.

After being released from captivity in Connecticut as part of a prisoner exchange in September 1778, William had moved to British-occupied New York, where he served as president of the Board of Associated Loyalists. In that role, he had sponsored a series of small but violent and deadly raids on American forces near Manhattan throughout the early 1780s. One of these included the lynching of an American captain. The lynching so outraged American colonials that William Franklin, fearing for his life, beat a hasty retreat to London. He arrived there in September 1782. The elder Franklin believed his son to be an embarrassment and, more importantly, a traitor. Complicating matters further was word that Shelburne had actually met with William, promising to do all he could to help the Loyalist cause.

At the negotiating table, Benjamin Franklin cloaked his personal rage in a fable. There was once, he said, a great lion king of the forest who had, among his subjects, a group of faithful dogs. The lion king was influenced by "evil counselors," and so one day went to war with the dogs. A few of them were of a mongrel race, derived from a mixture of wolves and foxes, and those dogs became corrupted by royal promises of great rewards. They deserted the honest dogs and joined the lion king in his tyranny. After the good dogs had finally won their freedom, the wolves and foxes of the lion king's council gathered to argue for compensation for the mongrels who had remained loyal to the lion king. But a horse rose up "with a boldness and freedom that became the noble of his nature," and argued that any reward from murder was unjust and would lead only to further wars. Thus the council had sense

Benjamin Franklin's son, William, was a Loyalist who led a number of deadly raids against American forces in New York during the early 1780s. Benjamin perceived William to be a traitor and was against making restitution to those Loyalists who had their estates taken from them.

enough, Franklin said, to resolve that the traitorous dogs receive no compensation.

"Dr. Franklin," Adams noted in his journal, "is very staunch against the Tories [Loyalists], more decided on this point than Mr. Jay or myself." This turn of events was ironic, because in the past Adams had more than once accused Franklin of being untrustworthy as the relative of a high-ranking Loyalist.

Franklin's persistence proved a problem for Lord Shelburne, who had promised to aid other Loyalists besides William Franklin. Numerous Loyalist emigrants lived in Great Britain by that time, and they had the British public's sympathy. Shelburne believed his government might fall if he

ARTICLE II OF THE TREATY OF PARIS, 1783

And that all disputes which might arise in future on the subject of the boundaries of the said United States may be prevented, it is hereby agreed and declared, that the following are and shall be their boundaries, viz.; from the northwest angle of Nova Scotia, viz., that angle which is formed by a line drawn due north from the source of St. Croix River to the highlands; along the said highlands which divide those rivers that empty themselves into the river St. Lawrence, from those which fall into the Atlantic Ocean, to the northwesternmost head of Connecticut River; thence down along the middle of that river to the forty-fifth degree of north latitude; from thence by a line due west on said latitude until it strikes the river Iroquois or Cataraquy; thence along the middle of said river into Lake Ontario; through the middle of said lake until it strikes the communication by water between that lake and Lake Erie; thence along the middle of said communication into Lake Erie, through the middle of said lake until it arrives at the water communication between that lake and Lake Huron; thence along the middle of said water communication into Lake Huron, thence through the middle of said lake to . . . Lake Superior; thence through Lake Superior north-ward of the Isles Royal and Phelipeaux to the Long Lake; thence through the middle of said Long Lake [to] Lake of the Woods; thence came away from the bargaining table with nothing to satisfy their claims. Thus, on direct orders from London, Oswald and Strachey pushed on this topic until the very end of negotiations. But Franklin threatened to throw out the entire agreement over this one point. After weeks of wrangling and debate, Franklin went so far as to pull out the original piece of paper from months before, where he had noted that if

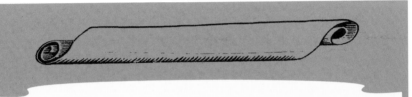

through the said lake to the most northwesternmost point thereof, and from thence on a due west course to the river Mississippi; thence by a line to be drawn along the middle of the . . . Mississippi until it shall intersect the northernmost part of the thirty-first degree of north latitude, South, by a line to be drawn due east from the determination of the line last mentioned in the latitude of thirty-one degrees of the equator, to the middle of the river Apalachicola or Catahouche; thence along the middle thereof to its junction with the Flint River, thence straight to the head of Saint Mary's River; and thence down along the middle of Saint Mary's River to the Atlantic Ocean; east, by a line to be drawn along the middle of the river Saint Croix, from its mouth in the Bay of Fundy to its source, and from its source directly north to the aforesaid highlands which divide the rivers that fall into the Atlantic Ocean from those which fall into the river Saint Lawrence; comprehending all islands within twenty leagues of any part of the shores of the United States, and lying between lines to be drawn due east from the points where the aforesaid boundaries between Nova Scotia on the one part and East Florida on the other shall, respectively, touch the Bay of Fundy and the Atlantic Ocean, excepting such islands as now are or heretofore have been within the limits of the said province of Nova Scotia.

Great Britain wanted compensation for Loyalists, it would have to pay for all the American towns savaged and goods stolen during the war, including Franklin's own looted Philadelphia library. Upon hearing this, Oswald and Strachey were forced to give in. They settled for a meaningless promise that Congress would "earnestly recommend" to each individual state that they compensate Loyalist estates confiscated within their borders. In the end, Franklin agreed to this soft language, while also insisting on one postscript aimed directly at his son, William: The recommendation was not to apply to any Loyalists who had taken up arms against America.

Ironically, on the very day Franklin told his tale of the dogs and the lion king, a gaunt Henry Laurens appeared at the bargaining table for the first time. David McCullough has described the starved and serious Laurens appearing almost as an apparition: "a stark reminder of the pain inflicted by a war that had still to end. To the lingering torments of his time in the Tower had been added the news that his son, Colonel John Laurens, had been killed in an unimportant action on a nameless battlefield in South Carolina almost a year after Yorktown. Laurens's one contribution to the proceedings was to provide a line to prevent the British army from 'carrying away any Negroes or other property' when withdrawing from America. Oswald, who had done business with Laurens in former years when they were both in the slave trade, readily agreed."

THE SEPARATE AND SECRET ARTICLE

The two sides also assented to "a separate and secret" article, which, it was agreed, would not immediately be made known to the French. This secret article dealt with Georgia's southern boundary west of the Chattahoochee River. The agreement stated that if Spain eventually allowed Great Britain to keep its holdings in Florida, the northern boundary of West Florida would continue along a line marked at latitude

32° 22' N stretching from the Chattahoochee River to the Mississippi River, just as it had before the American Revolution. On the other hand, if Spain insisted on the surrender of Great Britain's Florida holdings, then West Florida's northern boundary would go back to 31°N, as stated in the original 1763 Treaty of Paris. Neither Great Britain nor America consulted Spain on the language of this secret article. This proved a mistake, because Spain had plans to demand all of West Florida in return for its help in defeating the British. The resulting confusion stemming from the secret agreement would complicate U.S. relations with the Spanish until 1795, at which point Spain would finally agree to give up its claim to western Georgia north of the 31st parallel.

NOVEMBER 30, 1782

It was a Saturday when the parties met to sign the preliminary treaty: a day of yet another damp Paris snowfall. Oswald was the first to sign his name to the papers laid out on a table in his room at the Grand Hotel Muscovite. Then each of the three American commissioners, in alphabetical order, did the same.

Buying Peace

"You will notice," Charles de Vergennes wrote a colleague, "that the English buy the peace more than they make it. Their concessions, in fact, as much as to the boundaries as to the fisheries and the loyalists, exceed all that I should have thought possible. What can be the motive that could have brought terms so easy that they could have been interpreted as a kind of surrender [by the British?]"

VERGENNES INCENSED

Vergennes wrote those calm and cynical words only after he had time to simmer down. By negotiating a peace without the consultation and advice of Vergennes, the Americans had acted in direct violation of the French–American alliance. It was also against the commissioners' instructions from Congress to abide by the edicts of the French minister.

As far as Adams was concerned, the ethics of this situation amounted to nothing more than a hill of beans. Adams declared that Congress had "prostituted" itself by seeming to surrender sovereignty to the French. "It is glory to have broken such infamous orders," he wrote. "Infamous I say, for so they will be [known] to all posterity."

"I am at a loss, sir, to explain your conduct, and that of your colleagues in this occasion," Vergennes wrote stiffly to Franklin. After sending Vergennes a copy of the treaty's draft, Franklin called on him at Versailles one week later. In their conversation, Franklin stressed that the document was a draft, containing articles that had not been ratified. He likewise insisted—a bit untruthfully, given the points settled regarding the Grand Banks and the Mississippi River—that nothing had been agreed upon that went against French interests. To this Franklin added that no final treaty would be signed until the French and British had concluded their own talks. At that point, definitive, complimentary treaties would be signed by *all* parties.

"In not consulting you before [the preliminary articles] were signed," Franklin told Vergennes, "we have been guilty of neglecting a point of *bienseance* [propriety]. But, as this was not from want of respect for the [French] King, whom we all love and honor, we hope it will be excused, and that the great work, which has hitherto been so happily conducted, is so nearly brought to perfections, and is so glorious to his reign, will not be ruined by a single indiscretion of ours."

Later on, during the same audience, the audacious Franklin actually had the nerve to ask Vergennes for yet another French loan. "The English, I just now learn, flatter themselves they have already divided us," Franklin said. "I hope this little misunderstanding will therefore be kept a secret, and that they will find themselves totally mistaken." The best way to prove the British wrong, of course, was for the French Court to continue to extend credit—and, indeed, to significantly expand the credit—to the Americans, and to do so promptly.

On November 30, 1782, British and American delegates signed a preliminary treaty at the Grand Hotel Muscovite in Paris. The French were excluded from this treaty, but Benjamin Franklin assured them that nothing would be official until *all* parties signed a treaty.

Franklin's audacity paid off. The "little misunderstanding" was overcome in a matter of days. Vergennes approved one more loan, and then quickly got to work negotiating his own accord with the British. France signed preliminary articles of peace with Great Britain on January 20, 1783. The next morning, Franklin wrote Robert Livingston: "The preliminaries of peace between France and Spain and England were yesterday signed, and a cessation of arms agreed to by the ministers of those powers, and by us in behalf of the United States, of which act, so far as relates to us, I enclose a copy." At the signing (held in the Palace of Versailles), Adams and Franklin signed for the Americans, because Jay had gone to Normandy (in France) for his health and Laurens had gone to Bath (France) for the same purpose.

ARTICLES V, VI, AND VII
OF THE TREATY OF PARIS, 1783

Article V

Congress shall earnestly recommend it to the legislatures of the respective states to provide for the restitution of all estates, rights, and properties, which have been confiscated belonging to real British subjects; and also of the estates, rights, and properties of persons resident in districts in the possession on his Majesty's arms and who have not borne arms against the said United States. And that persons of any other description shall have free liberty to go to any part or parts of any of the thirteen United States and therein to remain twelve months unmolested in their endeavors to obtain the restitution of such of their estates, rights, and properties as may have been confiscated; . . . Congress shall also earnestly recommend to the several states a reconsideration and revision of all acts or laws regarding the premises, so as to render the said laws or acts perfectly consistent not only with justice and equity but with that spirit of conciliation which on the return of the blessings of peace should universally prevail. . . . Congress shall also earnestly recommend to the several states that the estates, rights, and properties, of such last mentioned persons shall be restored to them. . . .

And it is agreed that all persons who have any interest in confiscated lands, either by debts, marriage settlements, or otherwise, shall meet with no lawful impediment in the prosecution of their just rights.

(continues)

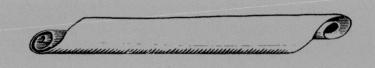

(continues)

Article VI

That there shall be no future confiscations made nor any prosecutions commenced against any person or persons for, or by
reason of, the part which he or they may have taken in the
present war, and that no person shall on that account suffer any
future loss or damage, either in his person, liberty, or property;
and that those who may be in confinement on such charges
at the time of the ratification of the treaty in America shall be
immediately set at liberty, and the prosecutions so commenced
be discontinued.

Article VII

There shall be a firm and perpetual peace between his Britannic
Majesty and the said states, and between the subjects of the
one and the citizens of the other, wherefore all hostilities both
by sea and land shall from henceforth cease. All prisoners on
both sides shall be set at liberty, and his Britannic Majesty
shall with all convenient speed, and without causing any
destruction, or carrying away any Negroes or other property of
the American inhabitants, withdraw all his armies, garrisons,
and fleets from the said United States, and from every post,
place, and harbor within the same; leaving in all fortifications,
the American artillery that may be therein; and shall also order
and cause all archives, records, deeds, and papers belonging
to any of the said states, or their citizens, which in the course
of the war may have fallen into the hands of his officers, to be
forthwith restored and delivered to the proper states and persons to whom they belong.

FRANKLIN'S NERVOUSNESS ABOUT THE FUTURE

And so the preliminary articles of peace between the United States and Great Britain were signed. But Benjamin Franklin—who in more positive moods had predicted a grand Anglo-American Imperium in the decades to come—turned darker and expressed his fear that a few years of peace might again lead to conflict between the two powers. Thus, unwittingly, he predicted a war he would never live to see: the War of 1812.

> A few years of peace, well improved, will restore and increase our strength but our future safety will depend on our union and our virtue. Britain will be long watching for advantages to recover what she has lost. If we do not convince the world that we are a nation to be depended on for fidelity in treaties, if we appear negligent in paying our debts, and ungrateful to those who have served and befriended us, our reputation and all the strength it is capable of procuring will be lost, and fresh attacks upon us will be encouraged and promoted by better prospects of success. Let us, therefore, beware of being lulled into a dangerous security, and of being both enervated and impoverished by luxury; of being weakened by internal contentions and divisions; of being shamefully extravagant in contracting private debts, while we are backward in discharging honorably those of the public; of neglect in military exercises and discipline, and in providing stores of arms and munitions of war to be ready on occasion; for all these are circumstances that give confidence to enemies and diffidence to friends; and the expenses required to prevent a war are much lighter than those that will, if not prevented, be absolutely necessary to maintain it.

Elsewhere, Franklin wrote: "All wars are follies, very expensive, and very mischievous ones. When will mankind be convinced of this, and agree to settle their differences by arbitration? Were they to do it, even by the cast of a die, it would be better than by fighting and destroying each other."

ADAMS SUMMING UP

Just as the preliminary Treaty of Paris was being sent to the United States for consideration and approval by the Continental Congress, John Adams reflected on his recent diplomatic adventures in his journal:

> I will venture to say, however feebly I may have acted my part, or whatever mistakes I may have committed, yet the situations I have been in, between angry nations and more angry factions, have been some of the most singular and interesting that ever happened to any man. The fury of enemies as well as of elements, the subtlety and arrogance of allies and, what has been worse than all, the jealousy, envy and little pranks of friends and co-patriots, would be one of the most instructive lessons in morals and politics that ever was committed to paper.

In order to provide his friends in Congress with a complete account of the peace negotiations, and especially to put his own role in the most positive light, Adams had relevant portions of his journal copied, those parts containing his day-to-day narrative of discussions. At first he intended to send this to one of the Massachusetts delegates, Jonathan Jackson. But then, upon consideration, he decided to direct it to the attention of Robert Livingston in an official packet containing official papers. The inclusion of the diary would appear to have been a mistake, but would nevertheless place Adams's personal observations in the hands of one of the most powerful men in Congress.

Debate and
Ratification

The Continental Congress met at Philadelphia during the winter of 1783. The matter of considering an agreement negotiated without the active participation of France was partially smoothed—even before the draft treaty arrived in North America—by an urgent letter from John Jay. The American diplomat presented Congress with an intercepted communication from Charles de Vergennes in which the French minister disputed America's claim to the fishing waters off Newfoundland, called it unreasonable, and suggested that France would not recognize such rights. In the same confidential message, Vergennes indicated that it might be a good idea to allow the British to keep border posts in North America after the peace, because this would make the United States continually dependent upon France for protection. As noted by James Madison—previously a firm friend

James Madison, who later became the fourth president of the United States, was a longtime supporter of France. However, he thought that some of France's demands within the framework of the Treaty of Paris were unreasonable. For example, France thought that it should hold fishing rights in the rich waters off Newfoundland.

of the French—"the tenor of it, with the comments of Mr. Jay, affected deeply the sentiments of Congress with regard to France." In France's defense, however, Madison added:

> Candor will suggest . . . that the situation in France is and
> has been extremely perplexing. The object of her blood and
> money was not only independence but the commerce and

gratitude of America; the commerce to render independence the more useful, the gratitude to render the commerce more permanent. It was necessary therefore, she supposed, that America should be exposed to the cruelties of her enemies and be made sensible of her own weaknesses in order to be grateful to the hand that relieved her.

Congress began debate soon thereafter on a motion to exempt the American commissioners "from the obligation to conform to the advice of France." The debate on this motion was heated. In the end, a majority of the members voted against a change in instructions. It was felt that such a change at such a late hour would reflect poorly on the good faith between America and its longtime ally. The motion, though not voted down, was postponed. A short while later, a letter from the French king expressed confidence that Congress would reject any proposal for a separate peace. This did much to rekindle warm feelings for France, and Congress unanimously approved a reply that stood by its original opinion. The response of Congress, recalled Madison, showed that the effects of Jay's letter did not last long.

TREATY DEBATE IN CONGRESS

This debate over changing the commissioners' instructions had just ended when Livingston received the signed preliminary treaty between the United States and Great Britain. Coincidentally, the same mail also brought a letter from Vergennes complaining of the "great indelicacy" with which he had been treated by the American representatives. In passing the treaty on to Congress, Livingston also passed on his own heated criticism of the American ministers' conduct, especially with regard to the secret article.

The disclosure that the American ministers had acted without consulting Vergennes, and that they had drafted language unfavorable to French interests, made for heated debate in Congress. The pro-French faction was furious that the American commissioners ignored strict instructions. As for the secret article—still not yet disclosed to Vergennes—that was the clearest breach of the American negotiators' orders, and it drew the heaviest criticism.

Representative John Francis Mercer of Virginia worked himself up into an out-and-out rage. "The conduct of our ministers throughout, particularly in giving in writing everything called for by the British expressive of disgust to France, was a mixture of follies which had no example, was a tragedy to America and a comedy to all the world besides." Mercer said he felt "inexpressible indignation at their meanly stooping, as it were, to lick the dust from the feet of a nation whose hands were still dyed with the blood of their fellow citizens." Mercer added that the American commissioners had shown "chicane and low cunning. . . . They proved that America had at once all the follies of youth and all the vices of age." Other delegates believed the commissioners had done a superb job. Eliphalet Dyer, of Connecticut, said he "fully approved of every step taken by our ministers, as well as towards Great Britain as towards France."

But the secret article was seen by almost everyone as a serious embarrassment. Eventually, a committee recommended that the American ministers "be thanked for their zeal and services in negotiating the preliminary articles" and "that they be instructed to make a communication of the separate article to the Court of France in such a way as would best get over the concealment." Worry and argument over the secret clause was still ongoing when Congress received word, in early March 1783, that the groundwork for the general peace had been signed on January 20. This news quieted any further discussion of the main terms of the Anglo–American treaty, although the question of the secret article still stood.

It was not until April that Livingston, acting at the request of Congress, wrote to the commissioners. He diplomatically congratulated them on the terms of the treaty and told of Congress's approval for those terms. Then he reprimanded the commissioners for conducting negotiations without consulting the French, and for signing the preliminary articles without first revealing them to Vergennes. "The concealment was, in my opinion, absolutely unnecessary," he wrote.

THE COMMISSIONERS WAIT

Diplomatic activity came to a standstill in Paris while the commissioners waited for word from Congress on the preliminary articles of the treaty between the United States and Great Britain. The problem of Congress's lengthy debate was made worse by slow communications. Copies of the treaty had been dispatched the previous November on four different vessels sailing for American ports. By the middle of April, the commissioners still had no word as to the reception of the treaty. Nearly five months passed without response to the most important news sent across the Atlantic since the outbreak of the war. Adams, the gloomiest of the commissioners, complained bitterly in his diary about "the profound silence of Congress, and the total darkness in which we are left concerning their sentiments." This darkness was "very distressing" to the commissioners, and "very dangerous and injurious to the public."

To his wife, Abigail, he wrote: "Day after day, week after week, month after month, roll away and brung us no news. I am so weary of this idle, useless time that I don't know what to do with myself." He spent numerous evenings with Jay, with whom he shared a similar preference for a quiet lifestyle, and whom he had come to admire more than ever. "I shall never forget him or cease to love him while I live." The two men took their exercise together, spending many hours on horseback. Adams reported that they "trotted about the environs of Paris" and spoke of the United States, where both of their hearts laid.

Concerned about the fate of the preliminary articles of the treaty—and anxiously wishing to be appointed ambassador to Great Britain's Court of St. James's once the final treaty was concluded and ratified—Adams quickly grew impatient with the round of French diplomatic receptions. He also grew alarmed that spring when Shelburne's government fell, giving way to a government dominated by a strange alliance: Charles James Fox, the Whig champion of American independence, and Lord North, architect of Great Britain's disastrous colonial policy, and no friend of U.S. sovereignty. The government seemed confused from the start. Fox—perhaps to humor Lord North's supporters—pushed a vote in the House of Commons condemning the peace that Shelburne negotiated. But then he sent diplomat David Hartley, a friend to both Franklin and the American cause, to Paris. There Hartley solemnly assured the commissioners that Great Britain would honor the preliminary articles and bring matters to a swift conclusion. Going forward, Hartley was to stand in for Richard Oswald for the balance of discussions.

ADAMS RESPONDS TO LIVINGSTON

The commissioners were relieved to receive word of Congress's approval for the preliminary treaty. But they felt rejected by Livingston's scolding in his letter. Adams, as was his nature, took Livingston's criticism as a personal insult. He responded with several in-depth, personal letters.

Adams explained his beliefs that if the commissioners had given Vergennes the provisional treaty for approval, Vergennes would have demanded they not sign until France was done with its negotiations on behalf of itself, Spain, and Holland. Such a delay, Adams insisted, would have put the treaty at risk because the unstable government of Shelburne was about to fall. Indications were that the prime minister's successors would be much less inclined to be as favorable to the United States as Shelburne was.

A signatory of the Treaty of Paris, David Hartley replaced Richard Oswald as Great Britain's chief negotiator with the United States. In early September 1783, Hartley took it upon himself to formalize the treaty after he did not hear back from his superiors.

In that instance, the commissioners would have had the choice of signing in direct defiance of the French—a course that would have severely jeopardized French–American relations—or sitting tight while their excellent treaty was ripped to shreds by a new government in Great Britain. To Livingston, Adams explained that Fitzherbert had told him that the Count de Vergennes had "fifty times approached me for ceding the fisheries, and said it was ruining the English and French commerce both." It was not suspicion, it was certain knowledge that they were against us on the points of the

DAVID HARTLEY
(1732–1813)

Leading British Liberal and Inventor

David Hartley was perhaps the leading British liberal politician of his era and a strong opponent of British warfare in America. (He was also, coincidentally, the son of another, more famous David Hartley, the philosopher who lived from 1705 to 1757.) In step with the American Henry Laurens, Hartley believed that political separation between the United States and Great Britain need not involve the severing of cultural, historical, and spiritual ties. On another front, Hartley was a ferocious and articulate opponent of the slave trade throughout his life. Hartley entered Parliament in 1774. His career in the House of Commons lasted until 1784. During 1778, he wrote a very important document: a pamphlet entitled "Letters on the American War." In his pamphlet, Hartley accused the Crown of mistreating the colonies, and made a convincing argument for American independence. Hartley and Benjamin Franklin—both of them sharing interests in politics and science, and both of them being inventors—became close friends. They shared a correspondence that was to last until Franklin's death in 1790.

In about 1776, Hartley earned fame for his method of fire prevention in city buildings. Enormous crowds flocked to watch the experiments Hartley performed at the so-called "Fire House," which Hartley built on London's Putney Common. Hartley protected the house with what he called "fire-plates." He installed these iron plates to protect the support timbers in the house's upper floors, below the normal floor

Tories, fisheries, Mississippi and the Western country. The iron was struck in the few critical moments when it was a proper heat, and has been molded into a handsome vessel. If it had been suffered to cool, it would have flown in pieces

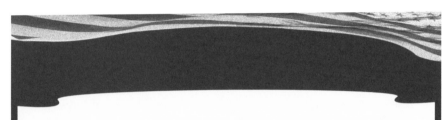

boarding. "The efficiency of the fire-plates," Hartley wrote, "depends partly upon their preventing the immediate access of the fire itself to the timbers of the house and partly on their preventing that exterior draught of air without which no house can be set on fire." It is said that at one of Hartley's demonstrations, King George III and Queen Charlotte calmly ate a meal on the upper story of the house while a violent fire raged below.

Eventually, after many such spectacular demonstrations at the Fire House, the town fathers of London passed legislation requiring that in all new buildings in the City, "the said Fire-Plates shall be ordered as part of the plan." Hartley went on to produce more advanced fire-proofing systems, using iron and copper plates both below and above floor support beams, and using sand between the timbers. In time, Parliament awarded Hartley funds with which to continue his research and invention. Years later, after the Fire House was no more, citizens erected an obelisk, which still stands, to commemorate its location.

Hartley's best likeness is a portrait done by his good friend Sir George Romney. The portrait depicts Hartley in a fur-lined coat not unlike the one worn so often by Hartley's friend Franklin. As more than one critic has commented, Hartley even seems to strike a pose reminiscent of contemporary portraits of Franklin. Hartley's connection with Franklin, and with America, is emphasized even more in the portrait by the presence of the Treaty of Paris, which lies rolled up on the table next to Hartley's outstretched hand.

like glass. Our countrymen have great reason to rejoice that they have obtained so good a peace when and as they did.

Adams said he just could not have the kind of confidence in the French, and their presumed goodwill, that Congress wanted him to have. "I must have been an idiot to have entertained such confidence," he said. Calling ingratitude "an odious vice," Adams explained that it was essential to distinguish "between those points for which we are not obliged to our allies from those which we are." Adams said he would always remain grateful for the loans, the troops, the fleets—but that France "had profited, too, in great measure by that aid." He added that France was

> a good-natured and humane nation, very respectable in arts, letters, arms and commerce, and, therefore, motives of interest, honor and convenience join themselves to those of friendship and gratitude to induce us to wish for the continuance of their friendship and alliance. . . . My voice and advice will, therefore, always be for discharging with the utmost fidelity, gratitude and exactness every obligation we are under to France, and for cultivating her friendship and alliance by all sorts of good offices.

But to be a worthy ally of the French, Adams concluded, Americans must be "manly," "honest," and "independent."

FINAL DETAILS

In talks during the spring of 1783, four American commissioners—Franklin, Jay, Adams, and Laurens—discussed fine points with Hartley. It was agreed that U.S. ports would be open to British merchant shipping as soon as British troops evacuated the United States. They also drew a careful road map for the removal of troops and so forth. Then Hartley sent all these details off to his government in London for approval. Seven weeks later, at the start of August, without having heard a single word of response from his superiors, an embarrassed Hartley took it upon himself to finalize the official treaty. In the absence of other instructions from his government, he simply repeated the provisional treaty of a year before without, as Adams put it, "addition or diminution." Although hoping for a more detailed document after all their work, the American commissioners seized the opportunity and signed. As Adams would recall, they realized that "all propositions for alternations in the provisional articles will be an endless discussion and that we must give more than we can hope to receive." Thus it worked to their advantage to take what they had. The signing took place on September 3, 1783.

Copies of the document were then sent back to the United States and England for final ratification by Congress and Parliament, with a pledge to exchange signed copies in Paris within six months. On January 14, 1784, Congress—with nine states represented—ratified the peace treaty. (New Jersey and New Hampshire had one delegate present. New York and Georgia were unrepresented.) Three separate couriers each rushed a copy of the ratified treaty to Paris. The first of these copies reached France in March 1784. Then on April 9, 1784, King George III himself personally ratified the treaty, five weeks after the formal deadline. Finally, on May 12, ratified copies of the treaty were exchanged in Paris.

SUMMING UP

"We have done our work well," Franklin wrote Jay. "We have discharged our duty as we saw it, and done well for both our country and for ourselves. If history will remember us at all, it may be because of this, do you not think? Does not the Good Book say 'Blessed are the peacemakers'? I would as soon be remembered as a peacemaker as anything else." To this Jay responded:

On September 3, 1783, representatives from Great Britain and the United States signed the Treaty of Paris. David Hartley, John Adams, Benjamin Franklin, and John Jay are depicted in this drawing.

We worked in strange but successful concert. We had in common, I think, good will and good sense. And between the three of us who did the most of this work—yourself, myself, and Mr. Adams—we combined to one efficient device serving well the interest of our countryman and, I would hope, mankind. Pride is of course a sign, but methinks I shall nevertheless be proud of my role here for some time to come.

The matter-of-fact Adams, for his part, claimed disinterest in how history remembered the commissioners. He fixed his eyes on more immediate concerns:

My prayer is that this peace will last at least so long that we who negotiated will not walk the earth to see it broken. I wish we could have hewn it better, and crafted a watertight vessel more capable of navigating the rough seas that inevitably lie ahead. It seems a good enough peace for now, on calm waters after the violent storm of revolution has passed. But I wonder how it will hold up when fast winds blow in rough weather once more? That is when we'll know how well we've wrought, and I fear we'll be seen to have come up short.

Constantly dissatisfied with himself and others, the conservative and domineering Adams was naturally inclined to look on the dark and pessimistic side of each and every issue. His fellow commissioners knew this full well. Thus they probably took his foreboding words in stride, and did not pay much attention. But in truth, both Jay and Adams would live to see another full-out war between Great Britain and the United States.

Nevertheless, the treaty shaped by Franklin, Jay, and Adams was the first in which a foreign government recognized the independence and sovereignty of the United States. That alone makes it as well crafted as it ever needed to be. That alone justifies and forgives it of any imagined or real shortcomings. Operating under imperfect circumstances, the American commissioners in Paris played the negotiating hand they were dealt, and played it well. In the final analysis, they achieved all that Congress had demanded of them, and more. They owe no apologies to the coming generations or to history. Quite the contrary, for it is they who are owed admiration, thanks, praise, and—last but not least—that most noble of titles: *peacemaker.*

Chronology

1775   **April** American Revolution begins.

1776   **July** Declaration of Independence.

1781   **March 15** General Charles Cornwallis clashes with General Nathanael Greene at Guilford Courthouse, North Carolina.

1781   **June** First Peace Commission (consisting of John Adams, John Jay, Benjamin Franklin, Henry Laurens, and Thomas Jefferson) is appointed.

1781   **September 15** French fleet drives British naval forces from the Chesapeake Bay.

1781   **October 19** American and French forces surround Cornwallis by land and sea at Yorktown, forcing him to surrender.

1782   **March 30** Lord North resigns as British prime minister, making way for the government of Lord Rockingham.

1782   **April** Franklin sends for John Jay and John Adams to join him, and then begins solo talks in Paris with British commissioners led by Richard Oswald.

1782   **June** John Jay arrives in Paris, and almost immediately falls ill for several weeks, leaving Franklin to continue negotiations.

1782   **July 1** Prime Minister Lord Rockingham dies and is replaced by Lord Shelburne.

1782   **August 1** Franklin takes ill, and the recovering Jay seizes the reins of negotiation for the Americans.

1782   **October 26** John Adams arrives in Paris; shortly after, he and Jay (somewhat reluctantly joined by

Franklin) open direct negotiations with the British without consulting French foreign minister Charles Gravier, count de Vergennes; this act is contrary to instructions from Congress; throughout November, they will meet almost daily with the British commissioners.

1782   **November 30** British and American commissioners (Benjamin Franklin, John Jay, John Adams, and Richard Oswald) sign preliminary Articles of Peace.

1783   **April 15** Congress ratifies Preliminary Articles of Peace.

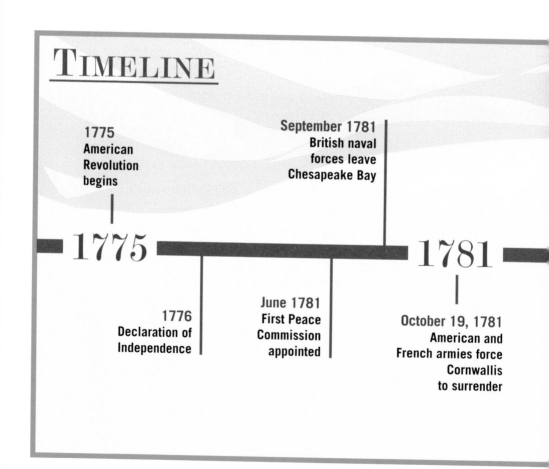

TIMELINE

1775
American
Revolution
begins

September 1781
British naval
forces leave
Chesapeake Bay

1775

1781

1776
Declaration of
Independence

June 1781
First Peace
Commission
appointed

October 19, 1781
American and
French armies force
Cornwallis
to surrender

1783   **September 3** Final Treaty of Paris is signed by John Adams, Benjamin Franklin, John Jay, and British commissioner David Hartley.

1783   **November 25** Last British troops leave New York.

1787   **September** U.S. Constitution ratitified.

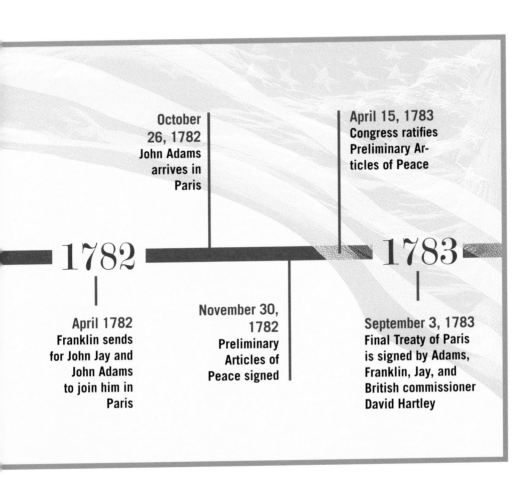

October 26, 1782 John Adams arrives in Paris

April 15, 1783 Congress ratifies Preliminary Articles of Peace

1782

1783

April 1782 Franklin sends for John Jay and John Adams to join him in Paris

November 30, 1782 Preliminary Articles of Peace signed

September 3, 1783 Final Treaty of Paris is signed by Adams, Franklin, Jay, and British commissioner David Hartley

BIBLIOGRAPHY

Brands, H. W. *The First American: The Life and Times of Benjamin Franklin.* New York: Doubleday, 2000.

Clark, Ronald W. *Benjamin Franklin: A Biography.* New York: Random House, 1983.

Dull, Jonathan R. *A Diplomatic History of the American Revolution.* New Haven, Conn.: Yale University Press, 1987.

Isaacson, Walter. *Benjamin Franklin: An American Life.* New York: Simon & Schuster, 2003.

Langguth, A. J. *Patriots: The Men Who Started the American Revolution.* New York: Simon & Schuster, 1988.

McCullough, David. *John Adams.* New York: Simon & Schuster, 2001.

Smith, Page. *John Adams, Volume 1, 1735–1784.* New York: Doubleday, 1962.

FURTHER READING

BOOKS

Hoffman, Ronald, and Peter J. Albert, eds. *Diplomacy and Revolution: The Franco-American Alliance of 1778.* Charlottesville: United States Capitol Historical Society, University Press of Virginia, 1981.

———. *Peace and the Peacemakers: The Treaty of 1783.* Charlottesville: United States Capitol Historical Society, University Press of Virginia, 1986.

Hutson, James H. *John Adams and the Diplomacy of the American Revolution.* Lexington: University Press of Kentucky, 1980.

Morris, Richard B. *The Peacemakers: The Great Powers and American Independence.* New York: Harper and Row, 1965.

Scott, H. M. *British Foreign Policy in the Age of the American Revolution.* Oxford: Clarendon Press, 1990.

Stinchcombe, William C. *The American Revolution and the French Alliance.* Syracuse, N.Y.: Syracuse University Press, 1969.

Stourzh, Gerald. *Benjamin Franklin and American Foreign Policy.* Chicago: University of Chicago Press, 1954.

WEB SITES

American Revolution Links at The History Place
http://www.historyplace.com/unitedstates/revolution/index.html

Liberty! American Revolution Links from PBS
http://www.pbs.org/ktca/liberty/

Essays on the American Revolution from Michigan State University
http://revolution.h-net.msu.edu/

Picture Credits

INDEX

About the Author

EDWARD J. RENEHAN JR., is the author of *Dark Genius of Wall Street, The Kennedys at War, The Lion's Pride, The Secret Six,* and *John Burroughs: An American Naturalist.* Renehan has appeared on C-SPAN, the History Channel, and PBS. He contributes to *American Heritage* and other national publications, and lives in coastal Rhode Island with his wife and two children.